Lead Your People to Go After Big Challenges, Not Each Other

SARAH THURBER & BLAIR MILLER PhD

GOOD TEAM BAD TEAM

PAGE TWO

Some names and identifying details have been
changed to protect the privacy of individuals.

Cataloguing in publication information is available
from Library and Archives Canada.
ISBN 978-1-77458-421-7 (paperback)
ISBN 978-1-77458-422-4 (ebook)

Page Two
pagetwo.com

Edited by Sarah Brohman
Copyedited by John Sweet
Proofread by Alison Strobel
Design and illustrations by Taysia Louie
Author headshots by Mary Rafferty;
all other photos by Doug Haight
Printed and bound in Canada by Friesens
Distributed in Canada by Raincoast Books
Distributed in the US and
internationally by Macmillan

24 25 26 27 28   5 4 3 2 1

goodteam-badteam.com

To the home team, Cole, Isabel, and Becca.
And to our FourSight partners, Gerard Puccio,
Greg Sonbuchner, and Russ Schoen.
You are all proof that life is better on a good team.

GOOD
TEAM
BAD
TEAM

Contents

Before We Begin

IN THIS BOOK, you'll find everything you need to lead a good team. It's our gift to you, our way to give back after decades of building our own successful companies and careers, equipping teams to think, connect, and solve problems together. We wish you the joy of being part of a good team.

Sarah Thurber and Blair Miller

INTRODUCTION
Drop Your Weapons

FIRST DISCOVERED team-building was a thing on a blind date. I had just turned thirty and was traveling the world as an independent freelance writer, editor, and designer. My friends, who occasionally described me as "the most single person I know," thought it might be time for me to settle down.

"You'll love Blair," said my friend who set up the date. "He's tall, smart, and handsome. He has a Master of Science in Creativity and does team-building for a living." I was dubious about the career choice but agreed to go on the basis of "tall, smart, and handsome." We went out for Thai food. By the time they cleared the noodle plates, I found myself leaning in, fascinated by Blair's insights into teams. Like any good freelance writer, I dropped into interview mode.

"How did you get into team-building?" I asked.

Blair had been a camp counselor, teacher, drama coach, and Outward Bound instructor. In graduate school, he had studied how to facilitate groups through complex problems. He rolled it all into a career as a team consultant.

"So, what happens in one of your team-building workshops?"

It was the mid-1990s, when trust falls and ropes courses were all the rage, and Blair was right on trend. He took teams out of their offices and gave them physical challenges they could overcome only by working together.

"Does it help?" I asked.

"It does," he said. "People find themselves in a new context, facing new challenges as a team. They start to see each other in a new way."

I must have looked skeptical.

"I remember one guy," he said, good-naturedly drawing me into a story. "He was a Vietnam vet who worked on a high-tech manufacturing team. On the first day of the workshop, I noticed him paying close attention when I read the 'Suggestions for Working Together.' The morning of the last day, he took me aside and confessed, 'I've worked with this team for years. This is the first day I've ever come to work without my knife.'"

"A knife?! Like, a *real* knife?" I stammered.

Blair laughed, delighted to have cracked my professional veneer. "I know. Crazy, right? But we're all hardwired for survival. For him, that knife was a symbol of self-protection. He'd brought it to work every day."

"He brought a knife to work?! For years? What made him stop?"

"He finally trusted his team," Blair said simply. "He had no reason to mistrust them before, but he didn't trust them either. The physical challenges we did together in the workshop showed him he could trust his team. So, he left his knife in the car."

Team-building was getting more interesting by the minute. Clearly, if you knew what you were doing, you could have a big impact on a team in a short time. If you could cause someone to stop carrying a physical weapon, what other emotional and intellectual armor could you get them to drop?

As a writer, you can always tell if someone is truly passionate about their subject. Blair practically glowed when he talked about teams. "People walk away from those workshops with new faith in their teams," he said proudly. Then he hesitated. "The problem is that the halo effect eventually wears off. People go back to work and fall into old habits. You can't expect companies to run outdoor team-building workshops every month. I wish you could!"

"So, what will you do?" I asked, a little concerned.

"I'm experimenting with a new approach. I've been wondering: Is it the trust falls and ropes courses that actually transform teams? Or is it the simple act of solving big challenges together?" He dedicated his graduate studies to finding out. He did research to see what had the biggest impact on teams. He found that the physical, experiential challenges he led in his outdoor workshops increased trust. The work-related problem solving he facilitated in meetings increased team cohesion and clarity. Why not combine the best of both?

That did it. Blair began to combine experiential activities with real-world problem solving. It became his signature style. He brought teams together around conference tables instead of ropes courses, and mixed creative problem solving with engaging group challenges.

"These days, I build teams by having them solve real problems," he said. "It's a win for the client. It's a win for the team. Sometimes, I miss the outdoor ropes courses and trust falls." He looked a little wistful. Then he cracked a conspiratorial grin. "Then again, my liability insurance got a whole lot cheaper."

After our first date, which Blair sometimes wryly refers to as "the interview," he became my favorite interview subject. We were married a year later.

Better Teams through Science
. . . .

Blair spent the next thirty years traveling the globe nonstop, supporting teams in Global 1000 companies. I called him the team whisperer. He trained and facilitated teams who had to innovate new products, solve problems, cut costs, develop strategic plans, and improve productivity. His unique approach helped companies make and save billions of dollars. Not millions. *Billions*. That's the impact good teams can have. Organizations that invest in good teams know that secret. The payback on good teams is rich.

During his career, Blair never stopped looking for new, research-based ways to unlock team performance. The biggest breakthrough came in the late 1990s when his friend Gerard Puccio, PhD, a professor at Blair's graduate program at SUNY Buffalo State University, discovered a scientific way to measure cognitive style differences. Gerard called them "thinking preferences." These thinking preferences could predict someone's behavior as they worked through a

This book will guide you on the journey to lead a good team. The upside is that if you follow this path, you'll soon be *on* a good team.

complex challenge. Gerard developed a valid, reliable self-assessment and called it the Problem-Solving Style Indicator (PSSI).

Blair immediately recognized its value to teams. "Gerard, my clients could really use this insight," he said, "but do you have to call the assessment the PISSY?" The two partnered on a business venture and renamed the assessment the FourSight Thinking Profile.

The FourSight assessment measures how people think—not how *well* they think, but how they *like* to think. With FourSight, you can anticipate how people will approach a challenge. You understand where their energy is likely to rise and fall as they work through it. Like any good assessment, FourSight gives the gift of self-awareness, helping people understand, *How do I approach a challenge?* Unlike other assessments, it also gives the gift of process-awareness, helping them understand, *What's the best way to approach a challenge?* Discovering your thinking preferences unlocks a common language for groups to solve problems.

When I married Blair, I was still living the independent life of a freelancer. A few years later, I was a wife, mother, business partner, and school volunteer. Suddenly, I was always on a team. Before long, I was asked to lead teams. I led committees, event teams, sports teams, and volunteer organizations. Knowing about thinking preferences gave me a distinct advantage. As a team leader, I knew what would energize people. I knew where they might get stuck. I knew where conflicts might arise and how to reduce them.

My publishing background came in handy at FourSight, where I helped to write, edit, design, and produce FourSight's first interpretive guide, which would ultimately be translated into nine languages and support collaborative problem solving in teams around the globe. In January 2010, Blair and Gerard asked me to lead the company as managing partner. I did what my years with FourSight had taught me to do: I built a good team.

That's easy to write.

It was hard to do.

Leading a good team didn't all come naturally. As you'll see in the next chapter, it came in fits and starts. Sometimes, it came kicking and screaming. Mostly it came from trying and failing, and finally applying the research-based insights you'll learn in this book. They are insights I learned not only from Blair, but also from team-building experts, researchers, and leaders around the world. Team-building was my business, and they were my clients.

Good Is the Goal

This book will guide you on the journey to lead a good team. The upside is that if you follow this path, you'll soon be *on* a good team.

Good is the goal. It was tempting to write about great teams or amazing teams. After all, who doesn't want an amazing team? By comparison, "good" seems apologetic. But think about this for a minute. If you had good health, a good relationship, a good living, a good home, good friends, good neighbors, a good education, good parents, and good kids, your "good" life would be amazing. Right? Who sold us the bill of goods that good isn't good enough?

As a mother of three, I suspect that much of the anxiety, depression, and isolation that plagues our kids stems from the fact that we dangle our "amazing" moments in front of everyone on social media and keep the "ho-hum" and "oh, crap!" moments to ourselves. Nobody can live up to amazing day in and day out. A good team doesn't worry too much about being amazing. Instead, they show up every day (or almost every day) and do the work, without fail (or nearly without fail). Life happens. So does failure. The point is that a good team isn't perfect. It's good, and that's what's so good about it. People on a good team know their purpose. They trust each other. They know how to solve challenges together. A good team can remain good for a long, long time and bring great joy and satisfaction to all the people it touches. It can deal with breakdowns and recover. And when it's called upon to be great, it can rise to the challenge.

Like many books about teams, this one has some familiar advice: lead with purpose, build trust, and work together to achieve goals. Here's what makes it different: *Good Team, Bad Team* draws on a proprietary database that contains over six million data points on cognitive diversity, collected through the FourSight Thinking Profile assessment. This data, and the research it inspired, will help you understand why people approach challenges so differently, and how they can work together with less conflict and achieve goals faster with better results.

Good Team, Bad Team is loaded with practical tips, science-driven insights, and real-world stories. The tips are proven, the insights are research based, and the stories are all true, though we have changed names and a few details to preserve the anonymity of our clients. The book unfolds in three parts.

1 **Know Yourself:** Discover your own problem-solving style so you can lead yourself and others more effectively.

2 **Know Your Team:** Learn how team purpose, trust, and climate can move the dial on collaboration, motivation, and performance.

3 **Know Your Challenge:** Share a common language to solve complex problems so your team can tackle any challenge.

This book will guide you to create a good team with the people you have. If you have a good team now, kudos. This book will help you understand *why* it's working and how to keep a good thing going. If not, take heart. A good team is something you can make on purpose. The ingredients are simple and if you combine them with care, authenticity, and compassion, the results are almost guaranteed. This approach works for multinational corporations, government agencies, start-ups, nonprofits, classrooms, clubs, and committees, as well as for remote, hybrid, and in-person teams. It even works for sports teams. Wherever groups of people commit to a common goal, this approach comes in handy. It will guide you to create a healthier, happier, more connected team. But chances are, you didn't come here just for that. You came looking for better results. Don't worry. You'll get those too. By the end of this book, you will know how to create a team that can focus its diverse problem-solving powers and together achieve unexpectedly good—dare we say amazing—results.

Part One

I think, therefore I am.

RENÉ DESCARTES

I know how I think,
and my whole team is so relieved!

SARAH THURBER

KNOW
YOURSELF

1

Your People Problem Starts with You

KNEW I shouldn't feel this way. I should be thrilled about my promotion to managing partner. I was leading the team. I had worked hard to get the promotion. I had years of publishing experience. I loved the work. I was good at the work. What no one around here seemed to understand was that I didn't exactly know how to *lead* the work. And I sure wasn't going to tell them now.

Leadership can be a lonely job. As with any job, there are some things you're good at and some things where you come up short. Now that I was the leader, I was a little reluctant to share my shortcomings. I didn't want to undermine people's confidence in me. So, I kept those shortcomings to myself and soldiered on.

The team I'd inherited was a disjointed group of people, all assigned to various tasks. They didn't know one another well, so most decisions came through me. I wanted to be a role model, so I tried to be a hands-on leader. No work was beneath me.

We need more customer service? I'll do it!

We need that shipped overnight? I'll drop it off!

I spent my days attending meetings, solving problems, fighting fires, fielding customer complaints, quelling rumors, shipping product, and pestering IT to make software fixes. I had no time to focus on the big goals the partners had set. My time was frittered away, coordinating work and solving people challenges. I thought these people were supposed to help me solve *my* challenges. I secretly missed my old job. It was so much simpler. Another email arrived in my inbox, another task to add to my to-do list. Should I delegate it? I sighed. I'll just do it myself. Other people just seem to complicate things.

IF YOU LEAD a team, you have two jobs. One is to achieve goals. The other is to support the people who help you achieve those goals. Both jobs are hard, but chances are you got the leadership role because you're good at getting things done. Achieving goals is your thing. What slows you down is managing other people's work, setting goals and expectations, and dealing with all the conflicts, disagreements, misalignment, miscommunication, and breakdowns that get in the way. Some days, you may spend more time dealing with people challenges than dealing with the challenges that would help you reach your goals.

You and every other team leader.

It's strange, really. Most leaders are trained to achieve goals, but not to lead teams. According to research from Gallup, team leaders are often chosen because they are high-performing individuals. We assume that high-performing people will lead high-performing teams.

I was a high performer—though I was definitely not leading a high-performing team. My progress was too slow. My plan to be a hands-on leader was failing miserably. At this rate, I'd never grow the business, never bring FourSight to the world, and never, ever go on another family vacation. Frankly, I'd never leave the office.

I had a people problem: I needed to clone myself.

Kelly, our bookkeeper, bailed me out. We shared a desk in the front office, and she could see I was in over my head. She offered to take over the customer service role while I went on vacation with my family. Bless her. Right away, it was clear that Kelly was better at the customer service job than I was. Much better. To be honest, I was a little surprised. I think of myself as pretty capable, but Kelly quietly stepped up. She listened carefully to customers. She was more patient, more deliberate, and she identified their problems quickly and solved them with the tools at hand. How did she do that? Whenever I got on a call, I'd listen to the customer and come up with three new product

If you lead a team, you have two jobs. One is to achieve goals. The other is to support the people who help you achieve those goals.

ideas, which would distract me from the problem they were going on about.

I looked across the desk at Kelly and laughed. I should have known. The two of us were acting out our thinking preferences. The Four-Sight company, where I now served as managing partner, published the FourSight Thinking Profile, an assessment that could predict how someone would approach a challenge. Our research showed that some people (like Kelly) like to clarify the problem, while others (like me) like to come up with new ideas and implement them. Kelly is a whiz at customer service, not just because she is smart, but because she likes to clarify the problem. That's the kind of thinking you need in customer service. She can think like that all day. It gives her energy. It gives me a headache.

Watching Kelly breeze through her customer service work made me think that maybe, just maybe, what we needed was not more of *me*. Maybe what we needed was more of *us*. Maybe, instead of focusing so intensely on goals, I needed to focus on people—the people who could help me achieve those goals.

A Recipe for a Good Team

I needed to change my mental model of leadership. I needed to stop leading tasks and start leading people. I needed to spend less time obsessing over an endless to-do list and start to build a good team—a group of people who could combine their problem-solving superpowers to achieve the big goals we had for our company.

Now I had a strong desire to lead a good team, but still no clear idea how to do it. Fortunately for me, I was surrounded by team-building experts. I married one. And many of Blair's friends were also professional team coaches, facilitators, and trainers. Even my customers at FourSight were team experts, including Amy Climer, PhD, whose dissertation research revealed that productive teams need three things: a clear purpose, healthy team dynamics, and a shared problem-solving process.

If I could build a team like that, I could solve my people problem. Heck, if I could build a team with a clear purpose, healthy team dynamics, and a shared problem-solving process, those people could solve any problem.

I began by sharing the company's higher purpose with Kelly. Four-Sight helps people think better together so they can create better teams and better solutions. Then we talked about the purpose of our office team. Kelly was the one who articulated it: we wanted to make FourSight easy for clients to learn, teach, and apply. I asked if she'd be willing to lead customer service permanently, and she agreed. She liked the challenge of adding a customer-facing role to her book-keeping job.

With customer service in good hands, I could finally attend to the challenge that was keeping me up at night. The software that ran our online assessment appeared to be buckling under the multiple features and updates we kept tacking on to the original code. Even its creators didn't know how to fix it anymore.

This was bad. If the code went down, our business would go down with it. The IT company we had contracted was capable, but not committed to our higher purpose. I had to find someone who could rebuild the code from the ground up and commit to the team, not just the task. This would be my first big hire.

The first candidate I interviewed was Chaz. We'd worked together before, and I knew he was smart, confident, inventive, and funny. We had the same FourSight Thinking Profile (something we'll unravel in the next chapter), so, not surprisingly, we had the same approach to the challenge.

"We can do this fast!" he assured me. "We'll lock ourselves in a room and figure out the specifications of the new system. We could be done planning in two weeks, and I'll start coding."

I liked the sound of that. Done! Fast! But a small voice in my head wondered if our mutual need for speed might cause us to skip over some of the finer points. The last thing I needed was a slapdash piece of code that we'd have to fix later. We'd tried that already. Twice. We had to get this one right.

The best way to solve
your people challenge is
**to build a team that
can solve any challenge.**

Then I interviewed Greg. He didn't promise me he could fix things in two weeks. He said it would probably take a year. His description of what needed to happen sounded far less exciting, but far more accurate.

I hired Greg. His FourSight Thinking Profile turned out to be completely different from mine, but both of us were committed to the team's purpose. It took him a year to build a new system, but he was true to his word. He built a rock-solid, enterprise-ready platform that thought of everything. It was one of the best investments—and one of the best hires—I ever made for FourSight, and Greg eventually became not only an IT partner and thinking partner, but ultimately an equal business partner.

I was getting better at building a team of diverse thinkers. Together, we were getting better business results. The new online assessment attracted more customers. As revenues grew, we grew the team. We added Diane in sales, Peter in marketing, and Russ in training. We were now a team of diverse thinkers who shared a problem-solving language and were aligned with a common purpose. People were well suited to their jobs and knew each other, so they could accomplish their work without me. That meant I could elevate my focus to goals, not tasks.

We certified hundreds of facilitators and published the FourSight Thinking Profile in nine languages. We supported tens of thousands of teams from corporate C-suites to manufacturing floors, from innovative R & D teams to combat teams, from students to social impact entrepreneurs. We grew the FourSight company sixfold and helped teams around the world think better together, including our team.

Here's what I wish someone had told me when I first got promoted: To lead a good team, being a high performer is not enough. Being highly motivated is not enough. Being an expert is not enough. Although those things are great, they miss the point. If you want to lead a good team, you have to solve your people challenge. And the best way to solve your people challenge is to build a team that can solve any challenge.

AS I SIT at the same corner desk across from Kelly today, I never would have guessed that what I would come to love most about my job was my team. My learning curve to lead a good team was an uphill climb, and still is. To be honest, I think "uphill" is simply the nature of any leadership path.

Leaders make a huge difference on a team. Think of a good team you've been on. What was the leader like? How did having that particular leader make you feel? What did you do as a result?

Think of a bad team you've been on. What was the leader like? How did having that person as a leader make you feel? What did you do as a result?

On the following pages, you'll see the responses we typically hear to these questions. They'll remind you why leading a good team is always worth the effort.

If you lead a team, you may have started out the way I did, proud, flattered, confident, and a little starstruck. Maybe those feelings got crowded out by insecurity, confusion, overwhelm, paralysis, and a little panic. If you stayed the course, maybe your confidence grew back, but perhaps you were still frustrated that things weren't better, that the team wasn't better, that you weren't better.

Without guidance, I never would have seen the path forward. But I was one of the lucky ones. My path was illuminated by world-class guides. I was surrounded by professional leadership coaches, team trainers, and problem-solving facilitators. I worked every day with clients who serve teams and with researchers who seek new knowledge about what makes teams work. I got all the mentoring, encouragement, and insights I needed to lead a good team.

This book is an effort to give it all back, to be a guide for other high performers who have landed themselves in leadership positions and want to do the job well but don't exactly know how. The next chapter will help you discover why you—and every other leader—breeze through some aspects of leadership and run smack into others.

Hint: The fault is not in your character. It's all in your head.

· ·

ACTIVITY
Download the Action Guide

· ·

BEFORE YOU START the next chapter, do something to guarantee a return on your investment in reading this book. Download the free action guide at foursightonline.com/good-team-action-guide. It's the fastest way to put these insights to work.

GOOD TEAM

WHAT WAS THE LEADER LIKE?	WHAT DID YOU DO?	HOW DID YOU FEEL?
Clear expectations	Worked hard ✓	Proud
High standards ✗	Took on challenges	Motivated
(Trusted)	Mentored others	Committed ✗
Interested in each team member	Showed loyalty	Empowered
Set big challenges	Shared resources	Connected
Hard-working	Communicated	Encouraged
Effective problem solver	Emulated leader	Respected
Supportive	Pushed myself	Confident
Good listener ✓	Exceeded expectations	Trusted
Team advocate	Rarely missed work	Purposeful
Self-aware	Put the team first	Productive
Good-humored	Learned so much	Valued
Genuine	Achieved big goals ✗	(Happy)
		Appreciated

BAD TEAM

WHAT WAS THE LEADER LIKE?	WHAT DID YOU DO?	HOW DID YOU FEEL?
Inconsistent	Complained	Incapable
Unsupportive (circled)	Missed work	Frustrated (circled)
Reactive	Kissed up	Used
Rude (crossed out)	Cut quality of work (struck through)	Mistrusted
Micromanaging	Kept my head down	Discouraged ←
Inflexible	Covered my ass (underlined)	Alone !!
Self-centered	Waited for the day to end	Self-doubting
Indecisive	Kept secrets	Resentful
"Fire! Ready! Aim!"	Avoided confrontation	Suspicious (underlined)
Demanding (circled)	Gave up (crossed out)	Demotivated
Unapproachable	Quit	Like quitting
Abusive (struck through)		

2

Trace Collaboration Breakdowns to the Source

EORGE WAS the new fire chief at the local station, and he needed to buy a new fire engine. He asked a rookie firefighter to make the purchase and was proud of himself for delegating the task. George had been a firefighter for twenty-five years, and he knew that purchasing a new fire engine would be a great way for the rookie to learn on the job. He'd have to interview his team members to learn what kind of truck would round out the fleet. He'd have to research the latest features available on the market. He'd have to weigh all the options carefully before making the purchase. The whole process would take the rookie a few months.

George was a little surprised when the rookie appeared at his desk a week later, looking pleased with himself.

"I've done it."

"Done what?" asked George, raising his eyebrows.

"I bought the fire engine."

"You did WHAT?!" George asked, trying to mask his shock.

"I bought the fire engine you asked me to purchase."

"How did you do it so fast?" George asked, feeling a little queasy.

The young firefighter beamed with pride. "I found our last purchase order and bought another truck just like it."

George hung his head. Not the result he wanted.

TEAMS EXIST to take on challenges too big for individuals to do alone. It's all good until people on your team start solving problems in ways that you find mystifying. You might ask yourself: What is this person thinking?! Let's take a closer look at that, because chances are your teammate is asking the same questions about you.

Wait, you might say, how is that possible when *their* thinking is the problem? Alas, the feeling is mutual. And the frustration is universal. I wish I were making this up, but I've got six million data points to prove it.

This chapter is about the science of thinking preferences. It will help you understand why people approach problems so differently. It will reveal the source of many collaboration miscues, so you can anticipate them sooner and fix them faster. It will also help you gain empathy for the people on your team. Once you understand thinking preferences, you can do more than just tolerate differences; you can see people's unique contributions and learn to leverage the cognitive diversity on your team to get better results.

The Real Tower of Babel

Thinking preferences are measurable differences in the way people like to approach a challenge. Until recently, we thought these were just irritating behaviors that made working with certain people a pain in the neck. Keep in mind, we all thought this. Meaning we all find it hard to work with people when our thinking preferences don't match.

This is a problem of biblical proportions. It exists across age, gender, nationality, race, creed, space, and time. For as long as people have been solving problems together, thinking preferences have made it harder. That is, until you understand those preferences. And when you do, all of a sudden, solving problems gets much easier.

Remember the Old Testament story of the Tower of Babel? The Babylonians got cocky and decided they would build a tower to the heavens. God got mad about this invasion of privacy, really mad. So God cursed humans by making them all speak different languages. Without a common language, the people couldn't collaborate. No teamwork? No tower. God didn't even have to knock it down. They just gave up.

I used to take that story literally. I thought humans had a linguistics problem. After working with FourSight data, I'm inclined to believe that the Tower of Babel was really the moment God cursed humans with thinking preferences. Because it can be a curse. The fact that we all want to solve problems differently has triggered many a collaboration crisis. It's all because we speak different problem-solving languages *in our heads.*

I bet you didn't know that. How could you? After all, everything you've ever thought happened in your head. It's familiar territory in there, the very definition of "normal."

In my early career as a freelance writer, I interviewed a forensic handwriting analyst. She had written a book on how to decipher people's personalities through their handwriting.

Interesting, I thought.

She worked in courtrooms and crime labs as a handwriting expert.

Legit, I thought.

I was impressed by her professional demeanor right up until the point where she analyzed my handwriting and told me that I was an "original" thinker.

Pfft!! I thought. She has no idea what she's talking about. I am definitely not an original thinker. I think like this all the time.

It's hard to imagine that other people could see the way we think as "different." Our thinking patterns come so naturally to us. They make so much sense. Yet, if you got behind the steering wheel in someone else's head, you'd find yourself traveling down some strange and unfamiliar roads.

The truth is, we all do think differently. But how differently? And differently from what? It's hard to know. It's like trying to look at your own eyes. You can't do it—not without a mirror. Likewise, you can't think (objectively) about your own thinking. You need something to provide an accurate reflection.

The Rosetta Stone of Problem Solving

This is where it pays to be close friends with a creativity nerd. Gerard Puccio, PhD, who prefers the term "social scientist," spent the better part of his career studying how people think. For thirty-five years, Gerard has been the chair of the Creativity and Change Leadership Department at Buffalo State University, part of the State University of New York (SUNY). His academic books, articles, and research have earned him the title of Distinguished Professor. In the early 1990s, long before he was distinguished, he stumbled on the phenomenon of thinking preferences.

His eureka moment happened midway through a workshop on creative problem solving. He was teaching a tool called the Evaluation Matrix—basically a visual spreadsheet that allows you to weigh your options. Gerard finished and sent people out on break. One woman approached him with her head in her hands. "I can't believe anyone thinks like that," she moaned. "That tool gave me a headache," she said, and left the room.

Gerard is a nice guy. Was it me? he wondered. A minute later, another participant came back from break and told Gerard, "I love that tool. That's exactly how I like to make my decisions!"

Two people. Two radically different reactions to the same problem-solving tool. Hmm . . . The social scientist in Gerard got curious. Was this a phenomenon you could measure?

He'd just published an academic book on psychological assessments. Maybe he could construct one of his own. His first attempts were promising, but imperfect. He kept at it. From the beginning, he wanted to measure problem-solving style, not ability. He wanted to identify people's problem-solving patterns and proclivities, their default modes and cognitive comfort zones. Six years and six iterations

For as long as people have been solving problems together, **thinking preferences have made it harder.**

of his assessment later, he nailed it. He could accurately predict how people would approach a complex problem. With thirty-six questions, he could scientifically measure thinking preferences.

Soon, it became clear that Gerard had come up with more than a companion piece to the MBTI, DISC, or StrengthsFinder. In fact, this was not a personality assessment at all, but a tactical way to improve collaboration in groups that were trying to solve problems together. By deciphering thinking preferences, he had discovered the Rosetta Stone of problem solving. His new assessment could translate people's internal problem-solving languages into a universal problem-solving process. His theory explained why people working on the same challenge often ended up working at cross-purposes. Their mystifying, boneheaded moves were nothing personal. They were simply thinking preferences at work.

Gerard's findings include some eye-opening insights on collaboration and problem solving. His research shows that

- you need four different types of thinking to solve a complex challenge.

- you probably prefer some over others.

- you like to work with people who share your thinking preferences.

  So, if left to your own devices,

- your solutions may come up short.

- you probably avoid the people who could help you most.

A (Really) Short Course on Thinking

To solve a complex problem, you need to call on these four types of thinking: clarify, ideate, develop, and implement. Put them together and they form the universal problem-solving process—the FourSight Framework. If you need a powerful solution, you need to tap all four.

Like a baseball diamond, you have to touch all the bases to get a home run. Let's take these four stages one at a time.

Clarify

When you clarify, you work to understand the challenge. You study it carefully and research it thoroughly to learn where it came from and why it exists. You ask questions to close information gaps and assemble a realistic picture. When you finish clarifying, you have a clear-eyed understanding of the problem you're trying to solve.

Ideate

When you ideate, you generate ideas. You power up your imagination and explore all the possibilities. You think outside the box, pushing past the obvious to come up with promising new ideas that address the challenge.

Develop

When you develop, you optimize the solution. You weigh ideas, find the best ones, and turn them into plans, keeping your success criteria in mind. The elegant solution you craft takes everyone and everything into account.

Implement

When you implement, you get into action. You see what needs to be done (and who needs to be convinced). Then you make it! Try it! Sell it! Do it! If it's a problem, you fix it. If it's an idea, you make it happen. If it's a plan, you act on it.

THERE YOU HAVE IT—the science of good thinking in under two hundred words. The FourSight Framework is simple. Of course, if it were that easy, this would be a very short book, and we could all go take a nap. The trouble is, this universal problem-solving process has one fatal flaw: users.

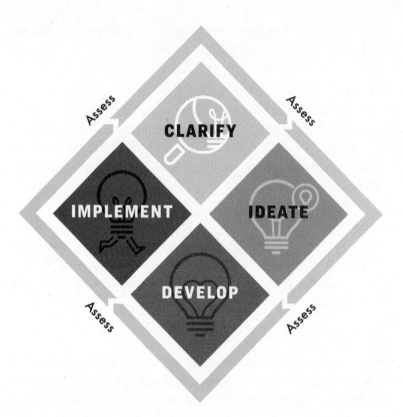

The FourSight Framework: This universal problem-solving process combines four types of thinking. The visual model was designed by Danish creativity expert Dorte Nielsen and Sarah Thurber, based on the work of Gerard Puccio and Blair Miller.

The Four Thinking Preferences

When humans try to solve problems together, our thinking preferences gum up the works. Gerard's research explains why.

People who prefer to clarify want to spend their time analyzing the problem. They tend to be factual, focused, orderly, deliberate, conscientious, and serious. They don't like to leap to conclusions. Instead, they want to gather all the facts and ask questions until they fully understand the situation. Sometimes, they suffer from "analysis paralysis."

People who prefer to ideate want to think big and imagine all the possibilities. They tend to be adventurous, independent, spontaneous, playful, social, and flexible. They prefer novelty over routine and like to think up ideas to solve a challenge. They see the big picture but not always the details. Sometimes, they get distracted by an idea. Then another. And another.

People who prefer to develop want to build the best solution. They tend to be reflective, cautious, pragmatic, structured, planful, and patient. They like to take time to consider and evaluate all the options and work out the details of their solution. Sometimes, they get stuck trying to develop the perfect solution.

People who prefer to implement like to make things happen. Right away. They tend to be persistent, decisive, determined, assertive, action oriented, self-starting, and unflappable. They translate "blah, blah, blah" into action steps. If others don't keep up, they take over. Sometimes, they rush to action too quickly.

PUT ALL these thinkers together and what do you get? Most of the time, you get a cognitive slugfest that looks something like this: Let's say you like to clarify. You go right for the facts. I like to ideate, and I go right for the ideas. My success strategy works for me. Yours works for you, but yours does *not* work for me. I find your deliberate, meticulous, cautious approach a little uptight. Okay, totally uptight. Devoid of any imagination. I feel as if you're creating the box that I can't wait to think outside of.

The discomfort is mutual. My freewheeling approach makes you nervous. You think, "She's jumping all over the place. Her ideas are so random. I don't even think she believes half of them." You're right. I don't. I need to spitball lots of ideas before I find a really good one. That's my success strategy. If you let me run with it, I'll come up with a great idea—something really original, just like the nice handwriting

Once you understand thinking preferences, you can do more than just tolerate differences; **you can leverage that diversity to get better results.**

lady said. But if you resist my approach, I'll start to resist *you* for interfering with my ability to add value to the team.

Instead of wrestling the problem, we'll start to wrestle each other.

Cue up the Tower of Babel soundtrack.

If you start with the premise that everyone thinks the way you do, the moment they think differently, you assume they're being slow or obstinate.

Thinking Preferences to the Rescue

This is where an understanding of thinking preferences can come in handy. When chronic collaboration breakdowns came to a boiling point on a local school board, consultant Teresa Lawrence, a former school superintendent herself, thought the FourSight Thinking Profile might help. She could see that the superintendent, who preferred to clarify, was always clashing with the board president, who preferred to implement. "When they planned their upcoming board meeting, the superintendent wanted to give all the background. The board president was like, 'Let's go!'" She continued, "When I showed them their thinking profiles, the board president turned to the superintendent and said, 'My God, I finally realize you're not trying to piss me off on purpose!'"

John Sedgwick, a psychology professor and FourSight practitioner, explains, "Human beings are label makers. The moment we meet, we try to identify whether someone is like us or not. If not, we tend to assign negative labels to those differences. Thinking preferences give us positive labels to understand the differences in how we approach a challenge."

Remember George, the fire chief? No doubt he had a few negative labels run through his head when that rookie announced he'd bought the fire truck. FourSight came to the team's rescue when leadership consultant Greg Buschman ran a FourSight workshop for the team. When George saw his rookie's thinking preferences, he shook his head ruefully. "I wish I'd known that six months ago," he said. "I would have given him different instructions." The rookie—who preferred to implement—bought the truck in record time. Problem solved. If

George had it to do over again, he would have told the rookie to clarify the station's needs, ideate on options, and develop a plan for George to review. If he had known the rookie's thinking preferences, George could have coached him to make a better purchase.

Like the rookie firefighter, most of us follow our problem-solving instincts. Our thinking preferences, left unmanaged, tend to produce conflict, resentment, and disappointing outcomes. When actively managed, they let ordinary people achieve extraordinary results.

The Argyle Team

Two business school friends—we'll call them Babs and Elena—were delighted when they got corporate jobs at the same company. One day their boss gave them a special assignment. "This is a problem we've tried and failed to solve many times," he said. "You've got three months."

Babs and Elena were eager to impress. When they had their first meeting, Babs launched right in. "Elena, I've been thinking a lot about this challenge. I thought of a thousand ways we could go about it. Then I had a big idea. It just hit me! It's so amazing. I actually started typing up the presentation slides. We're going to be done in half the time!" She beamed.

Elena nodded politely. "I've also been thinking about this challenge," she replied. "I went back to find the reports from past teams. In analyzing their findings, I realized they were focused on the wrong problem. They couldn't have solved it because they didn't have enough data. We have to do more research. It will take us twice as long, but I worked out a detailed plan. If we follow it step by step, we can solve this."

You would have thought Elena had just canceled Babs's birthday. Babs had burst into the meeting with her big idea, ready for action, and Elena wanted to do more research, follow a detailed schedule, and miss the deadline! What could be worse? But they were friends, so they tried to respect each other's input.

They wrestled constantly over where to focus and what was important. Finally, they finished. Their manager was so impressed, he gave them another project (not the outcome they'd hoped for). Over time, Babs and Elena gained a reputation as the dynamic duo of the division. Together, they could solve anything.

One day, Blair ran a team workshop and gave them their FourSight Thinking Profiles. Babs and Elena burst out laughing when they compared their results.

"Look! We're total opposites. This explains everything!"

Their graphs were like opposite zigzags. Where Babs's was high, Elena's was low, and vice versa. If you put their graphs together, it would have looked like an argyle sock. More importantly, when they put their *heads* together, they could solve nearly any challenge. By sheer dumb luck, one or the other of them had a strong preference for each stage of the problem-solving process. Every step of the way, someone brought energy and focus. They made an effective team, but it required a strong friendship to keep them collaborating.

Once Babs and Elena understood their thinking preferences, working together got easier. They still argued, but now they had positive labels to assign to their differences. It gave them confidence to know that the other was bringing something important—something they were missing—to the problem-solving process. They now understood the source of their collaboration conflicts. The other person wasn't trying to be difficult; they were trying to contribute in their own way. By understanding thinking preferences, they could see they were stronger together.

Once you understand that thinking preferences exist, you can begin to spot them in the wild. You can begin to translate other people's mystifying behavior into something that makes sense. No more Tower of Babel. You recognize someone's different thinking preferences as an asset. After all, they like doing a type of thinking you don't. If you work together, you're more likely to get a home-run solution. You don't need to find your perfect argyle, like Babs and Elena. You can leverage any difference in thinking preference.

When it comes to thinking preferences, knowledge is power. Ten minutes ago—before you knew how they worked—you had to ascend to a higher spiritual plane to be at peace with other people's thinking preferences. Now, through the handy lens of FourSight, you can see how their annoying behavior is not intended to piss you off. In fact, it could be their superpower in disguise.

ARE YOU CURIOUS to figure out your own thinking preferences? The best way is to take the FourSight Thinking Profile assessment at foursightonline.com/team-assessment. But for a rough idea (and for free), take the following quiz, originally published in the *New York Times*. That way, in the next chapter, when we look at how thinking preferences affect the way you lead your team, you'll be ready.

• •

ACTIVITY
What's Your Thinking Preference?

• •

GRAB A PIECE of paper and a pen and list the letter for the answer that best describes you in each question.

1 I'm most motivated by...
   a a need to get a clear understanding of the facts.
   b a great idea.
   c an opportunity to perfect an existing solution.
   d a job to do.

2 I learn best through...
   a facts, research, data.
   b stories, ideas, concepts.
   c evaluating options.
   d trying things out.

3 I like to spend time...
   a working with information.
   b imagining new possibilities.
   c making things "just right."
   d getting things done.

Score: How many times did you answer *a*, *b*, c, or *d*? If any letter got two or more points, it may correspond to a thinking preference for you.

Mostly a's—Clarify: You tend to be a cautious, structured thinker who likes to gather data to understand the reality and to identify problems, gaps, and opportunities.

Mostly b's—Ideate: You tend to be a playful, original thinker who likes to see the "big picture" and make new connections that might break the paradigm.

Mostly c's—Develop: You tend to be a detailed planner who likes to evaluate and perfect the best version of a solution and anticipate how it will move forward with the most success.

Mostly d's—Implement: You tend to be an action-oriented, confident risk-taker who likes to learn by doing.

About half of us have a single thinking preference. Others have two or three. Almost 20 percent have equal preferences for all four. Those are the Integrators, the people who tend to move smoothly through the process and focus on group harmony (more about them in Chapter 4).

3

Go from "Hands-On" to "Hands-In" Leadership

AS A LEADER, your thinking preferences are your superpower. Right up until they become your kryptonite. Letitia was your classic high achiever. She left her career as a top salesperson at a Fortune 500 company when she had kids and started to volunteer at their school. That's where we met. Every day, I pulled up to the carpool line riding a bike with a trailer and wearing whatever-doesn't-smell-or-have-spots-on-it. Letitia pulled up in her BMW, wearing designer sportswear. She had it together. When she was asked to chair the school marketing committee, no one was surprised.

Letitia liked her fellow volunteers, but they lacked her drive for results. Most of them were volunteering in order to meet other moms. Letitia was there to get things done. For her, the tasks were easy and familiar. She took a "hands-on" approach. She took over projects that dragged and finished work that was incomplete. She felt energized every time she crossed something off her list. But she didn't notice that instead of being grateful, her team was getting miffed.

One friend confided in me. "Letitia's kind of taking over. She seems to want to do everything on the marketing committee. Fine with me. I'm happy to let her do it." My friend started to show up late, then to miss meetings altogether. She wasn't the only one. Other team members also disengaged. Before long, Letitia found herself doing the work of five people. Under those conditions, even capable, competent Letitia was overwhelmed. Her team had evaporated, but what could she do? They were all volunteers.

Compared with Letitia, I was a committed underachiever in the volunteering department. I was up to my eyeballs at home with three little kids and a traveling husband. When the call for volunteers went out, I begrudgingly signed up to be assistant to the head room parent for Ms. Young's first grade class. I thought I could handle that much.

Kim, our head room parent, knew the ropes. Imagine my dismay when, three weeks into the school year, Kim took me aside and said, "Listen. I just got a full-time job. I need you to take over as head room parent." I remember where I was standing. I was suddenly rooted to the spot. I must have looked ashen, because she patted me on the shoulder. "Don't worry," she said, leaning in and lowering her voice. "This job is easy. You just have to know how to do it." She had my attention. "There are a limited number of events to put on during the school year," she continued. "You don't have to run them all. You just need to sit down over coffee with Ms. Young and decide on the dates. Then assign each event to a different parent."

At that point, I must have given her a disapproving look. Wasn't she supposed to run all the events?

"Believe me," she insisted, "it's good for the other parents. It gets them involved in their kid's class. It's good for you too, because all you have to do is meet with Ms. Young once and watch the whole year unfold!"

This felt like cheating. But given my circumstances, I followed her advice to the letter.

It was brilliant. We had a banner year. Everyone was involved—parents, students, Ms. Young. We all loved it. We were a good team. The next year, I volunteered to be head room parent again. And the year after that. I followed Kim's advice every year, enlisting the help of lots of parents to get everyone involved. Before my kids finished grade school, I'd been voted president of the parent volunteer committee—twice.

By this time, Letitia and I had become fast friends and workout buddies. She was conditioning for a triathlon—of course she was. Ever the overachiever, Letitia had outgrown her role on the marketing committee. She told me she was being groomed to take over as president of the school board. Her term would begin in the fall. On weekends, we'd bike up along Chicago's North Shore. As I pedaled hard to keep up with her, Letitia and I talked about our families, our friends, and our jobs. I told her about the FourSight assessment.

"Do you think the assessment could help me in my upcoming leadership role?" Her voice, normally self-assured, was anxious. She was nervous about running the school board. It was a big job, and she wasn't entirely happy about the way the marketing committee had turned out. She was looking for a better way to lead.

"Yes! You should take the assessment," I replied.

Your Thinking Preference Is Showing

When you lead a team, you have goals to meet and people to manage. You have to give assignments, clarify roles, communicate vision, fix problems, build systems, track trends, set strategy, and put out countless large and small fires along the way. Oh, plus your own work.

There's no way to get it all done. So, you have to choose where to focus.

If you're not careful, your thinking preferences will choose for you. You'll naturally gravitate to work that aligns with your thinking preferences and skip work that doesn't.

A thinking preference can be a huge asset in your role as a leader. It's like your own problem-solving superpower. It gives you extra energy for certain types of work. Where your energy goes, your focus follows. See if you recognize any of these behaviors in the following table in your own leadership style.

Leaders who prefer to...	may focus on tasks that involve...	and value...	and have jobs in...
Clarify	facts, information, roles, research, structure, purpose, analyzing problems	good problem analysis	finance, purchasing, analytics, customer relations, management
Ideate	new initiatives, new products, future vision, big picture, exploring novel approaches	good ideas	advertising, design, innovation, consulting, R & D, executive roles
Develop	systems, optimization, flowcharts, reducing failure, SOPs, consistency, engineering the perfect solution	good solutions	IT, engineering, planning, project management, quality control
Implement	getting into action, deadlines, to-do lists, motivation, accountability, persistence, selling, learning as you go	good results	sales, operations, execution, being in charge

Leaders who prefer to clarify tend to focus on roles, structure, purpose, and defining current reality. They like to be organized and prepared, and to give clear directions. When a challenge arises, they clarify to be sure they're going to address the right problem. Then they'll spend time thinking it through. They are reliable, realistic leaders whose predictable behavior builds trust on teams. However, sometimes they get so caught up in the need to gather more information that progress grinds to a halt.

Leaders who prefer to ideate tend to focus on future visions, innovation, change, new products, original approaches, and grand gestures. They are fun, playful, imaginative, and full of surprises. They foster exploration, celebrate new ideas, and try new things. But eyes roll when they come back from the latest conference with a whole new business model or a shiny new idea that requires everyone to shift focus. Again.

Leaders who prefer to develop tend to focus on optimizing solutions that are consistent and compliant. They are meticulous and detail oriented, which sometimes causes them to be nitpicky when it comes to others' ideas. If they commit to a particular solution, they like to pursue it to perfection, giving it all their time and attention. Sometimes this narrowing of focus can end up dragging the whole team down a rabbit hole with diminishing returns.

Leaders who prefer to implement tend to focus on results. They like to get things done, and if others move too slowly, they may just do it themselves. They deal in deadlines, checklists, goals, and quotas. They are persistent, confident, and willing to try and fail and try again, and they like to be in charge. But if their preference to implement takes over, they can steamroll over others (and steamroll right past clarify, ideate, and develop) and act before things are fully thought out.

YOU MAY recognize yourself in one or more of these preferences. Again, most people have just one preference. Others have two or three. The most common thinking preference is implement. About 33 percent of people in the general population have implement as one of their thinking preferences. Here's the shocker: about 58 percent of leaders do.

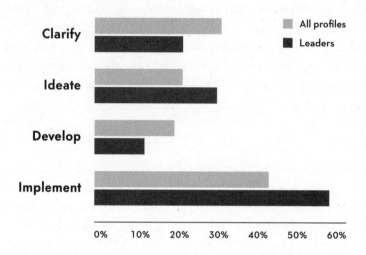

Thinking Preferences among Leaders: FourSight's review of more than 8,700 leaders—from supervisors to executives—revealed that leaders are almost twice as likely to prefer to implement than any other preference.

It makes sense. People who prefer to implement like to get results. They have a bias for action and an abundance of confidence, and they like to be in charge. Their can-do attitude and push for results means organizations will often put them in charge. That doesn't guarantee they'll be good leaders—that depends on their ability, not their thinking preference. In fact, many leaders have to overcome aspects of their Implementer preference to become good leaders.

The Power of "Hands-In"

When Letitia arrived at our offices, I handed her the results of her FourSight Thinking Profile. It was a one-page printout with a simple graph at the top and a short paragraph below.

"Look at the graph first," I instructed. "Those four dots show how much you prefer to clarify, ideate, develop, and implement. Those are

You'll naturally gravitate to work that aligns with your thinking preferences **and skip work that doesn't.**

the four types of thinking you need to solve a challenge. Now look at the line that connects the dots. That shows how your energy will ebb and flow as you work through the problem-solving process. It's like your own personal energy wave."

Letitia's graph looked like a giant checkmark. She had a low preference to clarify, an even lower preference to ideate, a slightly less low preference to develop, and soaring above the rest was a single high preference to implement. Letitia's FourSight profile was Implementer. This explained her laser focus on tasks. Letitia liked to get things done. She glanced at the graph and shrugged. "Yeah, that seems right."

"Read the description," I suggested.

Implementers like to make things happen. They are action oriented and take pride in getting things done, fast! Implementers have little patience for talk without action. They would rather spend their time creating a "to-do" list and checking things off.

Implementers are assertive, confident, decisive, determined, persuasive, and self-starting. With their seemingly boundless energy and drive, Implementers are open to taking risks and come across as unflappable and self-assured. When things seem to be going in circles, Implementers can move things forward. They can be honest to a fault and find it hard to hold back their views. The Implementer's challenge is impatience. Implementers may think that anyone not moving as fast as they are is not moving at all. Others may see Implementers as pushy, insensitive, domineering, or taking over.

In their drive for results, Implementers may speed past reflection, incubation, and analysis, making them vulnerable to solutions that are not fully formed or impulsive moves. Remember the carpenter's motto: "Measure twice, cut once." Implementers need to be sure that their strong desire to get things done doesn't get in the way of getting things done right. They should be careful not to oversell or to persuade others through sheer force of will, and instead use their powers of motivation to ensure that all the important work gets done.

Letitia finished reading and leaned back in her chair, looking a little stunned. "Well, that explains a lot." She reflected for a moment. "When

I ran the marketing committee, I guess I just took over. I got impatient at the pace things were going. I started doing the work myself."

Letitia is smart. It's one of the things I like about her. She understood where she fell down. On the marketing team, her preference to implement overcame her. Instead of relationships, she focused on tasks. Instead of working with people, she bulldozed over them. If people couldn't keep up, so be it—she'd do the work herself. But no one can keep up with Letitia. (Have I mentioned how fast she bikes?) When someone is constantly outpacing you, you start to feel like a plodder. When they take over your work, you get the distinct impression they don't think you're up to the task. You wonder if, indeed, you *are* up to the task. From there, it's a slippery slope to quiet quitting.

When Letitia read the description of her FourSight Thinking Profile, she got the memo. She didn't want to lead another disengaged team and relive the stress and isolation she felt as marketing chair. It had been miserable—for her and everyone else. She sat up straight and said, "I want to do my next leadership role differently. Do you think it's possible?"

"Totally possible," I said. "I was once right where you are. I get what you're up against. I prefer to implement too."

"Really?" She looked surprised. "How do you create such a strong sense of community? Your volunteers are so committed."

"I built that community by design," I said. I told her the story. Once, I worked with a guy named Joe, a Harvard grad, who used to walk into the library and pull random books off the shelf to read them. One day, he was paging through a book about the human hand and saw a small black-and-white photograph from the 1950s. It depicted a bunch of guys huddled over a car engine with their sleeves rolled up. They were up to their elbows in grease. The book explained: *community is created by putting hands in.*

Letitia paused, not seeing the connection.

"That's it. That's the secret," I said. "Get people to roll up their sleeves and put their hands in. Ask them to contribute. Give them a challenging task that fits their skills. The more elbow grease, the better. That's what creates a sense of community."

Give them a challenging task that fits their skills.

The more elbow grease, the better.

Letitia started taking notes.

I continued, "My mother-in-law did it by throwing potluck dinners instead of formal dinner parties. She said, 'When you throw a potluck, everyone shows up, because they're responsible for bringing part of the meal, and they always have more fun.' When people feel needed, they want to contribute. When they contribute, they feel part of something bigger. It's a virtuous cycle. That's the strategy behind everything we do on the parent volunteer committee."

The "hands-in" strategy was so obvious to me now. I'd seen it work over and over, as a parent, a coach, a volunteer leader. But it's not obvious to all leaders, especially "hands-on" leaders who prefer to implement. They have often risen through the ranks, winning praise for their ability to get things done. "Hands-on" is their thing. "Hands-in" is an entirely new move. Not only is it new, it's also slower, messier, and less reliable. You have to relinquish some control. You have to let others exert some authority. Things don't always work out as you imagined or march to your timetable. You have to be patient.

No wonder Implementers avoid "hands-in." They like speed. They like control. They like to set tasks up and knock them down. Sometimes they knock down people who get in the way. But hey, did you see how fast they got it done?!

Maybe you're like Letitia. You have a preference to implement. You've always considered it your superpower, but recently it has become your kryptonite. You try to delegate, but when others don't move fast enough, you just do it yourself. Taking over feels like the fastest way to get results. Yet as time passes, you see it erode community, undermine the team, and sap motivation. And you get stuck with all the work. That may not bother you, but it's bad for your organization. If you get hit by a bus, everything goes down with you.

If you find yourself spinning all the plates, keeping all the initiatives moving forward, leading all the projects, and doing all the tasks, it's time to give your preference to implement a good talking-to. Here's the good news. You'll fix it. You just have to put "learn to delegate (actually, really delegate)" on your to-do list. Then go after it with the same persistence you go after everything else.

Letitia did it. Armed with new self-knowledge, she transformed herself into a "hands-in" leader. She became president of the school board at a pivotal time in the school's history and successfully led the organization through some tough growing pains. Her secret: balancing her Implementer energy with creating community, developing others, and delegating. When Letitia was head of the school board, it was "hands-in" from the beginning.

. . . .

ACTIVITY
Self-Check-In for Leaders

. . . .

THERE ARE SIMPLE things you can do for your team to soften the impact of your thinking preferences. Try these tips.

For leaders who prefer to clarify

- Be aware that, when you ask too many questions, people may feel you doubt them. Reassure them that you are confident in their success and want to support their work.

- Notice the point at which you start to ask questions with diminishing returns.

- Sometimes, you've got to go forward without all the information, which may feel stressful.

- Be gentle with yourself as you increase your tolerance for ambiguity.

For leaders who prefer to ideate

- Resist the urge to articulate every idea that comes to mind. Write them down, think them through, and share them at a time that works for others.

- If you do share an idea, let people know: "This is just an idea, not a request."

- Stick with the agreed-upon plan. Resist the urge to run off after a new shiny object. Notice when your new idea is about to derail forward progress.

- When you share an abstract idea, be sure to concretize it with details and specifics so others can see it too.

For leaders who prefer to develop

- Make sure you are building a solution that others agree is solving the real problem.

- Let people know what you like about their work before you point out ways to improve it. That way, your constructive criticism won't just be heard as criticism.

- Agree on the level of resolution required, so your instinct to perfect things doesn't leave you trying to perfect every task, job, and project.

- Check with others to be sure your goals are as inspiring to them as they are to you.

For leaders who prefer to implement

- Remember: tasks are important, but people are just as important. Work to build relationships and trust.

- Act strategically. Be sure you are solving the right problem.

- Before you get to the gist of the meeting, take a moment to share the purpose, agenda, directions, or plan, so others can understand how to engage.

- Be patient. Other people may be solving the problem in ways you don't see.

For all leaders

- Create community by inviting others to contribute. Lead a "hands-in" team.

- Know the problem-solving superpowers of each person you lead.

- Know what kind of challenges will engage each individual and what they need to contribute their best to the team.

- Be responsible for your own thinking preferences. Recognize they can be an asset or a liability for your team.

· 4 ·

How Good
Leaders Think

A FAST-GROWING HR FIRM based in Sydney was stunned when revenues suddenly plummeted. LinkedIn had just entered the Australian market. The HR firm had heard of LinkedIn; the tech start-up had launched in the United States seven years earlier, but the firm's management team had been so focused on growing revenues, they hadn't given it much thought. Now, LinkedIn was posting job candidates on the Australian web, and their business was in jeopardy. The management team hired innovation consultant Dr. Ralph Kerle to help deal with the disruption.

Ralph gathered all forty-one managers of the HR firm into a room and began their session by giving them all the FourSight Thinking Profile. He wanted everyone to understand their thinking preferences before taking on a problem of this magnitude. First, they talked about individual thinking preferences. Then, he called for a show of hands to measure the team's thinking profile.

"How many people on this leadership team prefer to clarify?" Two hands went up.

"Ideate?" One hand went up.

"Develop?" No hands went up.

"Implement?" Thirty-eight hands went up.

Forty-one pairs of eyebrows went up. Was this normal? What did it mean?

"The revelation was a shock to everyone," said Ralph. "Almost every leader was an Implementer. It helped explain why no one had seen this market disruption coming." This team, as a collective, had such a strong preference to implement that no one had taken time to clarify market trends, ideate on possible disruptors, or develop a plan to address the risk. They'd all been busy implementing their current business model.

That's the hazard of homogeneity on a team when it comes to thinking preferences. Ralph coined a name for it. He called it "the blind spot phenomenon."

The Blind Spot Phenomenon

Teams reflect the combined thinking preferences of the individuals on them. Teams full of people with identical preferences often feel very compatible because everyone tends to focus on the same things and skip over the same things. It's great as long as you're one of the people whose thinking preference aligns with the majority. If you don't share your team's thinking preferences, however, you may feel ignored, dismissed, or even shunned.

As a leader, you have to be careful. You often have the power to hire, promote, and reward people who think like you—and fire those who don't. You can end up surrounding yourself with people who share your thinking preferences. The next thing you know, you may fall victim to the blind spot phenomenon.

In graduate school, my classmate Cat grew enamored of the Four-Sight assessment and decided to bring it back to the island where she lived off the coast of South Carolina. "I'm dying to give it to the board of directors of our Island Conservancy," she said. "They're kind of an insular group. I want to see how they think!"

Cat's own thinking preferences were to ideate and implement. I knew that once she got an idea in her head, there was no stopping her. So, off she went to South Carolina. She called in a panic two weeks later. "They all have the same profile!" she said in alarm. "It looks like they all have equal preferences for all four types of thinking! Is that common?!"

"It's common for a few people on a team to have that profile. We call it the Integrator profile." I explained that Integrators tend to move through the problem-solving process with steady energy, making sure everyone's voice is heard and every stage of the process is covered. Instead of focusing on one type of thinking or another, they tend to emphasize group harmony. "Roughly one in six people have that profile," I said. "What surprises me is that all six people share exactly the same profile."

"Maybe the technology glitched," she suggested dramatically.

"I don't think so, Cat. Tell me more about this group."

"They're very compatible. They get along incredibly well and seem to do the work of governing with very little friction."

"You definitely could be describing a whole group of Integrators," I observed. "The question is, what happens when somebody with a different thinking profile tries to collaborate with them?"

Cat started to laugh. "Well, I can tell you how they make me feel. With my high preference to ideate and implement, I feel like a revolutionary in there, throwing ideas around. They think I'm a real firebrand, trying to push my ideas through."

"It sounds like your board of directors really is made up of Integrators," I said. "Their shared thinking profile makes it easy for them to get along, but it seems hard for anyone else to break into their leadership circle."

Cat had encountered another example of the blind spot phenomenon in action. The only known cure is self-awareness.

Teaching Awareness

Dorte Nielsen, founder of the Center for Creative Thinking in Copenhagen, gave the FourSight assessment to the faculty of a Danish high school. She gathered all the teachers in the cafeteria, handed out their results, and asked them what they had learned from their thinking preferences. One teacher stood up and said, "I teach math, and I like to clarify. I've always thought my job was to pour as much information as possible into my students' heads. Now I realize that's just my preference. I have been boring three-quarters of my students to death."

Another teacher stood up. "Don't feel bad," she said. "I'm a social studies teacher, and I prefer to implement. Every time I give an assignment, the same five students come to my desk to ask questions about it. I tell them, 'Just jump in! Figure it out as you go!' Now I realize they must prefer to clarify. They actually need more direction to get started."

Turkish researcher Serap Gurak-Ozdemir found that the age-old concept of teacher's pet may actually be connected to thinking preferences. Serap found that teachers tend to look more favorably on students who share their thinking preferences. She gave 275 teachers the FourSight Thinking Profile and asked them to complete a checklist to describe their ideal student. Teachers overwhelmingly agreed on the same core character traits of honesty, kindness, and trustworthiness, but after that, she found their thinking preferences influenced their idea of who was an ideal student. Teachers who prefer to clarify idealized students who are prompt, organized, and serious (i.e., students who prefer to clarify). Teachers who prefer to ideate idealized students who are playful, imaginative, independent, and original (i.e., students who prefer to ideate). Teachers who prefer to develop idealized students who are earnest, cautious, and analytical (i.e., students who prefer to develop). Teachers who prefer to implement idealized students who are decisive, persistent, and action oriented (i.e., students who prefer to implement).

You can be sure that teachers aren't the only ones to play favorites. Leaders do it too.

When she works with corporate clients, Dorte, whose background is in advertising, uses the following graphic example to teach the blind spot phenomenon to corporate leaders. She flashes two FourSight group profiles on the screen. The first group clearly has a preference to clarify. The second group prefers to ideate.

"Think about how these two groups will get along," she says, challenging the leaders in her workshop to guess. "How will the clarify group see the ideate group?"

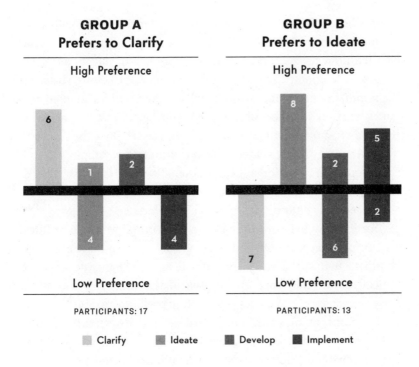

GROUP A
Prefers to Clarify

High Preference

Low Preference

PARTICIPANTS: 17

GROUP B
Prefers to Ideate

High Preference

Low Preference

PARTICIPANTS: 13

◻ Clarify   ◼ Ideate   ◼ Develop   ◼ Implement

Teams Have Thinking Preferences, Too: These group profiles show the number of people with high or low preferences to clarify, ideate, develop, or implement.

"As too playful. Not detailed enough. Disorganized. Not conscientious. Too imaginative," are often their answers.

"Right. That's just what the research tells us. And how will the ideate group likely see the clarify group?" asks Dorte.

"As too uptight. Too serious. Too cautious. Too rule-bound. Unimaginative," are the usual leaders' responses.

"Right again," she says.

Then Dorte does the big reveal. "These are real-life groups. The clarify group are students. The ideate group are their teachers." There is an audible gasp in the room.

Dorte then shares the unconscious assumptions of each group: The teachers thought their students would want to explore new, original approaches to the topic and would get bored by too many details or too much reading. But the students wanted nothing more than facts, detailed information, and a chance to ask lots of questions. Both groups were doomed to a miserable semester until Dorte revealed their thinking preferences. She recalls, "The teachers laughed out loud when they saw these profiles. One said, laughing, 'Ah, that's why they didn't enjoy dancing during the math class.'" Once the teachers understood how their students liked to think, they happily altered their approach to better suit the students' needs. Next year, they'd have to do it all over again because the new batch of students might have an entirely different set of thinking preferences.

Dorte shows her corporate clients the FourSight group profiles of their own departments and working teams. Often there are stark contrasts. In the creative agencies she serves, the finance department typically favors clarifying. The creative department prefers ideating. Account managers and media buyers often prefer to clarify and implement. The classic antipathy that often develops between those groups feels personal, but it's easily explained by thinking preferences. Before they understand thinking preferences, different departments may look on each other with suspicion, but by the time Dorte is finished with them, they see how everyone contributes to the whole.

Understanding thinking preferences makes things easier—easier for teams to work together, for teams to work with other teams, for leaders to work with their teams, and for teams to work with their leaders, as you'll see in the following story.

Would You Invest $100K?

Blair was hired by a Canadian financial services company to facilitate a new strategic plan. The young president was charismatic and visionary. In his short time as president, he'd already made a splash in the industry. His company made the cover of the nation's largest business magazine for its new, innovative financial products.

To prep for the session, Blair met one-on-one with the company's top leaders. He wanted to hear their ideas of where the company should focus in the next three years. Most were enthusiastic about the recent innovations but felt a need to balance innovations with back-office operations. Only the CFO, a seasoned veteran in the industry, was stonily firm. All these innovative products were glamorous and getting lots of media, he said, but they needed to spend the next three years shoring up operations to support them. Failure to do that would lead to ruin.

"Be sure you voice that in our upcoming session," Blair said.

"I won't be attending," said the CFO.

"We haven't solidified the dates yet," Blair said. "I'm sure we can accommodate your schedule."

"You don't understand," he said. "I'm not coming."

"Oh."

"I am crystal clear about what needs to happen to turn this company around," the CFO continued in a calm, steady voice. "I know what's going to happen in that session—more talk about new ideas and innovations. That'll sink us."

The CFO wasn't there when Blair kicked off the two-day strategic planning session. The young president was all smiles, looking forward to two days of future-focused thinking. An hour later, when Blair handed out people's FourSight Thinking Profiles, he noticed that the president's profile had a single high preference—to ideate.

The group spent the first day teasing out key initiatives that would take the company from its current state to the desired future vision. Despite the CFO's gloomy predictions, much talk did focus on operational efficiency and shoring up systems to support the new products. The president didn't seem to mind. At the close of the day, the president came over to Blair. In a congratulatory tone designed for everyone in the room to hear, he said, "Well, Blair, this has been an interesting exercise, but since this vision isn't going to make the company more innovative, I assume we will do the *real* vision tomorrow." Then he turned to the group. "Thank you, everybody, for coming. I look forward to seeing you bright and early tomorrow!"

He left behind a team of slack-jawed executives.

The next morning, one senior vice president showed up early.

"I couldn't sleep last night," he told Blair. "I kept thinking, if I had $100,000, would I invest it in this company? And I realized, if we

Following your instincts is not the surest path to leading a good team. **Knowing them is.**

carried out the new strategy we outlined yesterday, I'd say yes. If not . . ." he trailed off, and shook his head. "So, I called everyone on the leadership team. I asked them all the same question: If you had $100,000, would you invest it in this company? Everyone said the same thing: 'With our new strategy, yes. Without it, no.' What I'm trying to say is, I think this is a leadership moment. We need to confront the president."

Blair nodded. "I won't get in your way."

The president breezed in at the top of the hour. "I'm so excited!" he said. "Today, we're going to come up with a vision that will make us the most innovative financial institution in the country."

The room was strangely quiet. No one mirrored his enthusiasm. Then the senior vice president stood up. "With all due respect," he said, "I think we need to innovate by getting operational excellence under the new products we've just created. Some of these instruments are coming to maturation within two years, and we've got to be ready. We need to focus on operations."

The president was taken aback. He looked quickly around the room, waiting for someone to stand up in his defense. Another senior vice president did stand up. "You've been really successful at coming up with new ideas for this company, but it feels like you've got blinders on. You've got this thinking preference to ideate, and the only way you see us being innovative is to invent new products. We need to look at this from a broader perspective. We need to innovate by developing sustainable systems under those products."

Everyone watched the young president for his reaction. He stood at the podium, taking it in. For someone usually so suave and confident, he looked unsure. Then, he called for a break.

When he came back into the room fifteen minutes later, he looked chastened. "I agree with the team," he announced. He supported their desire to follow through with the strategy they had created the day before. Operations had won the day.

The team had used thinking preferences to frame this leader's unchecked penchant for new products as a thinking preference, not a personality flaw. Everyone saved face. The company was back on track to succeed, and no one lost their job that day.

After the meeting, Blair called the cynical CFO to report the outcome. He was very surprised—and very impressed.

Keep Your Ego—and Your Thinking Preference—in Check

Nobody steps up to a leadership position with the desire to screw it up. You want to be a good leader, to perform above average, and to win the hearts and minds of others. But let's face it, there's some ego involved. And that's not a bad thing. Ego can push you to strive for greatness, but ego is a fickle guide. Ego may convince you to defend your thinking preferences, to feel confident you are right when you should be curious why others don't agree.

The young president was confident. Why shouldn't he be? His preference to ideate had led the company to glory. It was a perfect match for the challenge he envisioned: How can we make this company even more innovative? But his leadership team, many of whom shared his preference to ideate, recognized that the real need was to develop those innovative ideas into solutions.

Their leader's thinking preference was out of step with what the company needed. The team saw it first. They needed to resist his instinct to follow his preference. As good stewards of the company, they needed to follow the problem-solving process instead. Their courage in standing up to him was half of what saved the day.

The other half was his response. He listened. He saw they were right. He recognized that his thinking preference had taken over. He changed course and allowed other types of thinking to emerge. He checked his ego and allowed other thinkers to help him lead in a more strategic direction.

Leading People Who Think Differently

We all have something to contribute to the problem-solving process. Discovering the thinking preferences on your team can make you a better leader. And if innovation is your goal, it can make you a more innovative one.

Helene Cahen, author of *Fire Up Innovation*, works with high-tech companies whose lifeblood is innovation. She uses the FourSight Thinking Profile and problem-solving framework to foster cognitive diversity and creative problem solving on teams. In her TEDx Talk, she poses a provocative question: "What if I told you that the Golden Rule—the one that says, 'Treat others the way you want to be treated'—can actually kill collaboration and innovation?"

We often think of diversity in terms of age, ethnicity, and gender, but a study by Alison Reynolds and David Lewis published in the March 2017 *Harvard Business Review* showed that cognitive diversity has the biggest impact on performance. In a strategic execution exercise, the researchers found that age, ethnicity, and gender didn't make a difference, but teams with cognitive diversity—a difference in perspective or information processing styles—performed significantly better than homogeneous ones.

Helene points out two obstacles that get in the way of leveraging cognitive diversity: 1) the fact that it's not visible, and 2) the fact that we unconsciously avoid it. As the blind spot phenomenon predicts, we often surround ourselves with people who think like us and avoid people who don't.

"FourSight makes thinking visible on teams," she says. "It teaches you to see others for who they are and embrace our differences in thinking. We need to leverage our uniqueness, rather than our uniformity, to be successful."

As a leader, you can feel vulnerable, even embarrassed, to admit that you have high and low thinking preferences. After all, others are relying on your good judgment. But here's my advice: be honest about your own thinking preferences. (Believe me, no one will be surprised.)

Give Clarifiers...	Give Ideators...	Give Developers...	Give Implementers...
Order	Room to be playful	Time and space to consider the options	Assurance that others moving just as quickly
The facts	Constant stimulation	A chance to evaluate	A sense of control
An understanding of history	Variety and change	The opportunity to develop ideas	Timely responses to their ideas
Access to information	The big picture		
Permission to ask questions			

I share an office with my team. I prefer to ideate and implement. I sometimes burst into the office with a new idea, ready to act on it. Sometimes this happens multiple times a day. Sometimes every five minutes. Suffice it to say, I have a lot of ideas, and I urgently want to implement them all.

When we hired Holli as our new office manager, it was obvious she didn't share my preference to ideate. Holli was a no-nonsense problem solver—buttoned-down, organized, and serious. In her last job, she'd run big corporate teams with big corporate budgets. After two weeks of sharing the front office with me, Holli took our bookkeeper, Kelly, to lunch and asked, "What do you do when Sarah keeps coming up with all those ideas?"

Kelly chuckled. "I've been sharing a desk with her for nearly a decade. She's just ideating," she told Holli. "Just ignore her unless she actually says your name." After lunch, Kelly couldn't wait to share their conversation. She told me with a twinkle in her eye.

"Really!? I do that?" I asked, covering my face with my hands. "I'm so sorry. That must be so irritating. Ugh! I promise I'll work on it."

We all had a good laugh. I thanked them for their feedback and thanked FourSight for giving us a language that allowed personal feedback to be offered in a way that didn't feel personal. Instead, it felt actionable.

I worked on my behavior, as promised. I still had the same number of ideas, but I began to notice the impact they had. I realized that, for my team, my off-the-cuff ideas often sounded like requests, not just ideas. I was more deliberate about the ideas I shared and when to share them. I tried to make them less abstract, concretizing ideas with examples and substantiating them with data.

Holli and I began to collaborate more frequently. Over time, she became my go-to person when the ideas in my head got stuck on spin cycle. I would show up at her desk. "Can we meet?" I would ask. "I'm stuck in ideating!" She would smile, nod knowingly, and start asking clarifying questions, helping me to focus the ideas and narrow down my to-do list. Rather than avoid each other, or tolerate each other, Holli and I became argyle thinking partners. We learned to appreciate each other's unique gifts and leverage our differences to produce remarkable results.

Overcome Your Blind Spots

Every thinking preference has upsides and downsides. As you become more aware, you can increase the upsides and reduce the downsides.

Clarify Upside	Clarify Downside
Asks clarifying questions	Asks too many questions
Understands the history	Overloads people with information
Gathers data to get a realistic picture	Needs proof for everything
Uses information to see gaps	Worries about what might go wrong
Identifies the right problem to solve	Focuses on data but misses the big picture
Thinks things through	Suffers from analysis paralysis

Ideate Upside	Ideate Downside
Comes up with ideas and possibilities	Gets distracted by a new idea
Sees the big picture	Misses the details
Challenges assumptions	Can't stop coming up with new ideas
Takes intuitive leaps	Disrupts the plan
Inspires others with vision	Is out of touch with reality

Develop Upside	Develop Downside
Weighs the options carefully	Takes forever to decide
Improves and strengthens ideas	Endlessly polishes the plan
Anticipates stakeholder needs	Nitpicks other people's ideas
Crafts workable solutions	Gets locked into one approach
Builds systems	Organizes obsessively

Implement Upside	Implement Downside
Gets into action	Acts before thinking it through
Is confident taking risks	Oversells the solution
Builds momentum for the team	Gets impatient with others
Learns as they go	Takes a "Fire! Ready! Aim!" approach
Focuses on results	Launches before it's ready

THE SECRET to overcoming the blind spot phenomenon is to know you *have* a blind spot; your own thinking preferences, if overplayed, can undermine your team. That's why *following* your instincts is not the surest path to leading a good team. *Knowing* them is.

Part One of this book has helped you to know yourself. Now that you understand thinking preferences and how they work, you can anticipate how you will approach a challenge and how to tap the energy of others as they engage differently.

Part Two shifts from self-awareness to team awareness. We will equip you with tools to clarify your team's purpose, build trust and psychological safety, and shepherd your team through the stormy cycle of team development, so you can create a productive team climate where everyone and every thinking preference can thrive.

GOOD
PREFERENCE

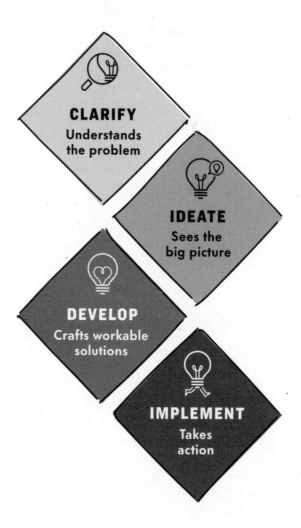

BAD PREFERENCE

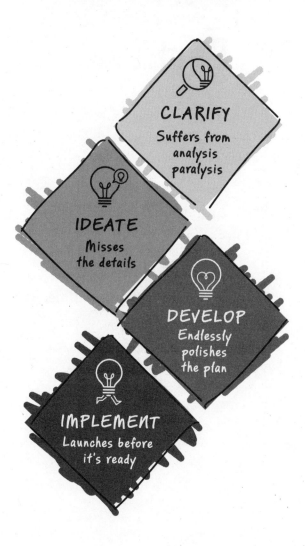

CLARIFY
Suffers from analysis paralysis

IDEATE
Misses the details

DEVELOP
Endlessly polishes the plan

IMPLEMENT
Launches before it's ready

Part Two

You may have the greatest bunch
of individual stars in the world, but
if they don't play together,
the club won't be worth a dime.

BABE RUTH

KNOW YOUR TEAM

• • 5 • •

Teams Work
on Purpose

ETIENNE WAS ecstatic when he got the promotion. He was now president of the division charged with bringing a new discovery to market. This once-in-a-lifetime opportunity had the potential to create a $1 billion product line for the company and rocket his career forward. He was honored to be chosen for the task.

But the glamour was fading fast as the immensity of the task presented itself. A foreign competitor had joined the ring. To be the first to market, Etienne would have to be awarded dozens of patents and win FDA approval in less than eighteen months. Arguably, that deadline was impossible, but he might just pull it off with a team of hard-charging experts. Instead, he was assigned a team of 150 mid-career workers, a collection of data scientists, chemists, legal experts, and marketers who had just survived five consecutive corporate reorganizations. These people knew how to keep their heads down, not stick their necks out.

Etienne looked at his prospects. He couldn't change the people on his team, but maybe he *could* change the way they worked together. If past experience had taught them to be cautious, conservative, and guarded, he would need to find a way to teach them to take risks, collaborate, meet impossible deadlines, and create breakthroughs. He was introduced to Blair by a mutual friend and liked the idea of combining classic team-building and creative problem solving. He hired

Blair as his team consultant, saying, "We need these people to work together like no team in this company has worked before."

Blair met Etienne's leadership team, the thirteen people who led the functional teams, at a monthly team leader update. They gathered in a poorly lit conference room in the old R & D facility. For two hours, one after another, the functional team leaders stood up and narrated highly technical PowerPoint slides to update progress in their area. "It was impressive," Blair recalls. "There were a lot of smart people in that room—PhDs, scientists, and experts with decades of experience. I left thinking, 'Wow, these guys really seem to have things under control.' But the truth was, I didn't understand half of what they said."

Blair wasn't the only one. Each functional leader had spoken in such specialized terms that no one understood anyone else, and no one wanted to be the first to admit it. But a billion-dollar opportunity was at stake. To meet their goal, these people would have to find a common language with which to work together.

Blair urged Etienne to host an all-team meeting. In preparation, he asked the functional team leaders to meet with their teams and identify three things: 1) their team purpose, 2) the key questions they were trying to answer, and 3) the animal mascot that best represented the team. "Explain it so everyone can understand how it contributes to the whole," he said. "Share it on a poster in the fewest possible words and in the simplest possible terms, as if you were explaining it to a ten-year-old." The new assignment raised some skeptical eyebrows. An animal mascot? Really? But no one said anything. These were professionals. It was a simple enough request.

On a Friday afternoon, Etienne's entire team of 150 members gathered in the R & D cafeteria. The walls were adorned with posters, each representing a different team. Each one had its own animal mascot and a clear statement of purpose.

Etienne kicked off the meeting. He was standing under a giant poster of a wooden boat filled with animals. His mascot was "the Ark." His team's big purpose: "When we go public, we'll be ready to go to market with a product that people want and patents that make it impossible for others to enter the field. My question is, how can I support you in this challenge so that each of you will gain skills and experience that enhance your career?"

That was it. No PowerPoints. No graphs. People looked up, stunned, as if Alexander the Great had marched into the room and sliced the Gordian knot in two with his sword. The team had spent weeks trying to untangle the complexity of this business challenge. The sheer simplicity of Etienne's approach was so audacious it brought hopeful smiles to people's faces. Their team's purpose was crystal clear.

The functional leaders stepped up next. Process engineering (the beavers) said their purpose was to refine ways to make the product. Their question was, "How do you make it fast and cheap?" Legal (the hawks) said their purpose was to protect the team's freedom to operate. Their question was, "How can we collaborate with customers, competitors, and partners, while still protecting that freedom?" Sensory research (the meercats) said their purpose was to ensure the product tasted good. Their question was, "How do you like it?"

And so it went down the line. The relief was palpable. Within an hour, the roomful of highly specialized technical experts was buzzing with excitement. Everyone understood each other's role. People crisscrossed the room, offering support and asking questions. With the purpose of every team clear, people knew how they could contribute.

Everyone was aboard the Ark.

After that meeting, Etienne's team became a hive of activity. People stopped each other in the hall to share ideas, collaborated across functions, and together created breakthroughs that resulted in a record-breaking number of patents and disclosures. Over the months that followed, Blair taught Etienne's team how to strengthen trust, climate, and creative problem solving, all things you'll learn about in upcoming chapters, but the first order of business had been to clarify the team purpose. Right on deadline, Etienne's team shipped their submission to the FDA for approval. Word came back from the FDA that the team had set a new gold standard for FDA submissions. Soon after, they won FDA approval, paving the way for commercial success.

What is your team's purpose? This is such a simple question that it is astonishing how many smart people forget to answer it, or even ask it.

What Is Your Team's Purpose?

A good team has a clear purpose. That sounds so simple, but bad teams often botch it. They never quite get around to establishing a clear purpose. Or they think it's so obvious, they don't bother to articulate it.

A team can operate without a clear purpose, just as a boat can sail without a rudder. It's possible, but it makes things harder. That rudderless boat is harder to steer and harder to navigate. It's harder to make progress and reach your goal. Also, your passengers will probably want to jump ship.

What is your team's purpose? This is such a simple question that it is astonishing how many smart people forget to answer it, or even ask it.

In her research on teams, Amy Climer, PhD, identified purpose as one of the three things a productive team needs. I called Amy to let her explain this in her own words.

"First, teams need to have a clear purpose: What are we doing together? Why do we exist?" she told me. For some teams, the answers to those questions are obvious. For example: "We're the marketing team. Our job is to let people know about this product."

For other teams, the answers are not obvious. Amy recalls, "I've asked executive teams what their team purpose was, and they could not answer my question. They looked confused. 'Do you mean the purpose of our organization?' they asked. 'No, that's your mission statement,' I told them. 'What's the purpose of this team? Why do you all meet every week or two?' I asked them. They couldn't answer that."

She continues, "Without a clear purpose, it's hard to know what work belongs to the team—what's a priority for the team and what isn't." Amy also says that the team's purpose has to be shared. "Everybody on the team needs to understand it, buy into it, and care about it. If the team leader knows the purpose but team members don't, that's not enough. If the team knew it once but has since forgotten, that's not enough."

What is your team's purpose? How do you state it? And if you asked everyone on the team, would they say the same thing?

Jerry Folz leads a Vistage team, a CEO peer group of a dozen or so business owners who meet every month to develop themselves as leaders, businesspeople, and humans. Every month, Jerry starts his team meeting the same way, by calling on the host to share the team's purpose. The host, often a new member, is invariably busy fussing over the bagels and making sure the coffee hasn't run out. Jerry's question jerks them to attention. Everyone else smiles knowingly, as they watch the host's eyes widen, scanning the room for clues. "Um . . . What is it again?" They're a little embarrassed to have forgotten the team purpose already.

"To help each other get better!" the group calls out in chorus. After a few meetings, the new member chants along. Reciting the team's purpose every month is Jerry's way of reminding the group where to focus: on each other. It's a simple device that helps a roomful of independent business owners feel more like a team.

Ready or Not, Time to Clarify

When Blair was eleven, he went to Camp Shewahmegon, a boys' camp in northern Wisconsin. He returned every summer until he was too old to be a camper, and then he joined the team of junior counselors. Bill Will, the camp director, was a military man turned educator. He knew his way around roles, assignments, and kids. The team of junior counselors had a clear purpose: to contribute to the camp community by taking care of the grounds and supporting the senior staff.

"He'd always give us special projects," Blair remembers fondly. "We mended fences, repaired roads, and resurfaced tennis courts." Given the job description, I was a little surprised he remembered it so fondly. The boys had precious little experience, but Bill Will (whose name was always spoken with reverence and always with both his first and last names) gave them clear directions, handed them the required equipment, and left them to do the job.

"When we finished, he'd come back to review our work," Blair says. "It was always a great day when he'd say, 'Job well done, boys!' We were so proud." Whether he knew it or not, Bill Will had tapped the secret to creating a highly motivated team. He gave them challenging work that helped them grow, a connection to their fellow counselors, and the autonomy to accomplish their tasks on their own.

When Blair came home at the end of the summer, it was his mom giving out assignments. She was an artist and her approach was more intuitive, less structured, and a whole lot more frustrating. "On a Saturday morning, when all I wanted to do was play with my friends, she'd say, 'Oh, Blair, I just remembered, could you please cut the lawn?' I'd say, fine, and I'd push the lawn mower around. As soon as I finished, she'd say, 'Oh, and could you trim those bushes?' I'd grumble and trim the bushes. 'Honey, could you put the trimmings into the yard bin? And while you're at it, could you do (insert random task here)?'" Blair felt as though her list would never end. When he finished one task, his mother had already sparked an idea for the next. He couldn't wait to leave the house, but he never felt good about leaving.

NOBODY FEELS GOOD when they fall short of expectations—even vague or unreasonable ones. Clarity of purpose protects both leaders and teams from that kind of failure by creating alignment, which builds trust and increases motivation. Bill Will knew that. He embodied the characteristics of a good leader. He also communicated clear expectations, had high standards, came prepared, gave his team big challenges, called for hands-in teamwork, and set the team up for success. The young men who were working for him felt inspired, motivated, committed, connected, trusted, purposeful, productive, and valued. So they worked hard, tackled big challenges, pushed themselves, exceeded expectations, put the team first, and learned a lot.

Blair's mother was a good person—a wonderful person—but she was a trained artist, not a trained leader. So she did what most untrained leaders do: she followed her instincts. She preferred to ideate, so she kept things fluid, flexible, and open. She wasn't trying to torment her son. She was just problem solving in the way that came most naturally to her.

Unfortunately, while making original artwork requires ideating, assigning yard work requires clarifying. She didn't know how to shift *thinking* gears. She just kept thinking up tasks, one after another, with no apparent rhyme or reason. Blair couldn't wait to go back to camp, where the purpose was clear, the tasks were defined, and team success was almost assured.

If you like to clarify, you have a distinct advantage when it comes to establishing your team's purpose, roles, goals, and strategies. Chances are, you've thought about those things already. Whereas those of us who avoid clarifying (no judgment) may have avoided pinning those things down. The connection between good clarifying and good teamwork is real. A research study by Gerard Puccio, Shiva Jahani, and Trisha Garwood revealed that leaders who prefer to clarify enjoy a higher level of trust among followers. That's partly because, when you're crystal clear on your expectations, roles, deadlines, and resources, people know what they need to do. They know what you expect. They know how to succeed at their work.

When someone doesn't meet your expectations, take a moment to reflect: What's at the root of the breakdown? Before you point the finger at someone else, ask yourself: Was it their lack of effort or my lack of clarity?

You don't have to like clarifying to lead a good team; you just have to do the clarifying work. One surefire way to do it is to draw up a team charter, which includes elements like purpose, time, scope, members, roles, resources, and deliverables. You can use the prompts at the end of this chapter or the template in your online workbook to make one. A team charter may feel a little prescriptive to those who don't prefer to clarify, but it sets team expectations and answers a lot of questions before they're even asked. It ensures that people don't spend more time wondering what they're supposed to be doing than actually doing it.

That's the practical side to clarifying purpose. There's also an inspirational side. You help people see how their daily tasks connect to higher goals that align with the greater vision, values, and mission of the organization. So, they know their work has meaning.

When someone doesn't meet your expectations, ask yourself: **Was it their lack of effort or my lack of clarity?**

Share Your Purpose Early and Often

Collaborating with clarity of purpose is like bowling with bumpers: it vastly increases your chance of knocking down the pins. But as soon as the bumpers disappear, it's back to gutter balls—at least in my bowling game.

After you read this chapter, I'm sure you'll remember to communicate your team's purpose whenever you launch a team. But that's not enough. Purpose has a shorter half-life than you'd expect. Unless you communicate it early and often, purpose loses its power to align teams.

Jonathan Vehar should have known better. He is a leadership coach, professional facilitator, and organizational development consultant. Midway through his career, he took a corporate job as head of product development for one of America's oldest leadership development companies. He was put in charge of a team responsible for developing and launching a new leadership course to add to the company's product lineup. He was told privately that recent launches had posted lackluster sales. Jonathan was determined that this one would be different.

In January, he assembled the team of trainers, subject-matter experts, marketers, and salespeople to talk about their team purpose. He wanted everyone to have a sense of ownership. Their agreed purpose was to launch two successful courses. They drew up a team charter to clarify what they were building, why they were building it, and how they would do the work.

Course development began strong and ran like clockwork right up until mid-April, at which point progress mysteriously stalled. Jonathan asked around to find out what had happened. He ran a purpose check with someone who had recently joined the team.

"So, why are we doing this?" he asked.

The guy gave him a blank stare. "I don't know. Is that a trick question?"

Then it struck Jonathan. This guy hadn't been part of the project launch. He didn't know the purpose of the team.

"He honestly didn't know," Jonathan recalls. "It's a little embarrassing. I'm the guy who is all about strategic direction, and I just missed it. People had lost track of the purpose." From that point forward, he started weekly meetings with the mission of the company and the purpose of the team.

"Do we really have to go through this *every* week?" someone complained.

"Yes," he replied. "Your purpose is your touchstone. When you make a difficult decision, ask yourself: If we do this, will it help us achieve our purpose? Then make your decision."

Jonathan's approach worked. The two courses his team launched were the most successful the company had seen in twenty years.

IT'S NEVER too late to clarify your team purpose, even if you've been together for years. Take time to articulate it. Do it together to drive alignment, create a sense of connection, and help everyone gauge what work belongs to the team. Whether you make a team charter or keep team purpose alive in a less formal way, remember that teams succeed on purpose. Without it, they flounder. With a clear purpose, you have paved the path to reach your goals.

Ask yourselves, Why do we exist?

Once your external purpose is clear, you're ready to focus on the internal relationships that will drive it. In the next chapter, we'll talk about building trust and psychological safety, which will help you carry out your team's purpose.

. . . .

ACTIVITY
How to Make a Team Charter

. . . .

A TEAM CHARTER is a handy tool to help a team get clear on its purpose, roles, scope, goals, communication—and anything else that needs clarifying. Use it to launch a new team, recharge an existing team, or onboard new team members. Get out your physical or digital whiteboard and build team commitment by answering these questions with your team.

Team purpose

Why does this team exist? Headline your purpose in five to ten words, then add your answers to the following questions: What issues does this team address? What are the expected outcomes from this team? Go ahead, make this bit inspiring. It will help later when people lose momentum.

Time commitment

How long will this team be together? What commitment of time is expected? How much time (daily/weekly/monthly) are people expected to work to fulfill the team purpose? Setting a realistic expectation of the time commitment involved lets everyone plan accordingly.

Scope

What work will this team accomplish? What marks the beginning and end? The more clearly you can define what is in and out of scope, the less likely the team is to suffer from scope creep.

Members and their roles

Who's on the team, and what do they do? To help people connect, list the name, contact information, and skills of each team member. Articulate roles, responsibilities, and sub-teams as appropriate. Know each other's thinking preferences.

Stakeholders/sponsors

Whom do we work for—and with? Who is the end user of our work? What other groups (both internal and external) will we collaborate with? To whom are we accountable?

The result you want

What are the deliverables of this team? What are our goals and their relative importance? What is the quality of our output? What key performance indicators (KPIs) will measure success?

Resources

What will support our work? What communication platforms will we use? Who outside of the team will support us? List other resources; for example, meeting rooms, budget, and software.

Procedures and commitments

How will we work together? How will we make decisions? How will we handle breakdowns? How will we handle differing levels of commitment? What suggestions will we follow for working together? (See Chapter 8.)

Communication plan

How will we communicate progress? How frequently do we report on our progress, and what needs to be included? Where will work be posted and shared? How often will we report to our key stakeholders/sponsors?

GOOD PURPOSE

BAD
PURPOSE

6

Trust Me

SHYLA RAN a team of young biomedical engineers whose job was to travel the country supporting clinical trials for a multinational medical device. The team took an intensive, six-month onboarding crash course online. Zooming in from all corners of the country, a cohort of six new hires studied together, encouraged one another, and created a bond of trust. These engineers loved being a small part of a big operation. They knew their work had a higher purpose—they were improving health care. They knew their team had a clear purpose—they were supporting clinical trials. They were proud to be part of the team.

A year after the new hires started work, the company came under fire. Stock prices dropped. Salaries froze. Promotions froze. Apparently, Shyla froze. She hesitated to share the bad news coming down from corporate. She started to communicate with individuals only on a need-to-know basis, leaving the rest of the team in the dark. What she failed to realize was that the team were still close and met weekly on their own Zoom call. It didn't take them long to realize that Shyla was feeding different information to different people.

"Why isn't she straight with us?" complained Aditi, one of the team's top performers. "How can she not protect us from this kind of organizational nonsense?" Before long, their trust in Shyla had dissolved completely, and nearly every new hire started looking for another job.

When the first one quit during his annual review, Shyla panicked. It had taken months to train these people. The good ones were hard to replace. She called Aditi. "You're not leaving in the next month too, are you?"

"No," Aditi answered truthfully. Aditi was leaving in five weeks—which was technically more than a month away. She knew her departure would create hardship for Shyla, but she was only willing to share that information on a need-to-know basis.

Shyla's story reveals that team trust follows the laws of physics: whatever you give them, they give you back in equal and opposite measure.

Trust is a key ingredient of a healthy team dynamic. As a leader, you can earn people's trust quickly, but you can lose it just as quickly. Are you being straight with your team? Are you transparent about what you know, don't know, and can't share? No one expects you to divulge organizational trade secrets, but people do expect you to communicate honestly and openly.

How Leaders Build Trust

In 2017, researcher Paul J. Zak published a book on the neuroscience of trust called *Trust Factor*. It shows that trust is not simply an abstract virtue. Trust is a belief whose presence produces a physical change in the brain. Zak chose to measure levels of oxytocin to identify what activities contributed to trust. Then he compared people in high-trust and low-trust companies.

After ten years of research and thousands of employee surveys, Zak found that people who worked at high-trust companies reported

- 74 percent less stress
- 106 percent more energy at work
- 50 percent higher productivity
- 13 percent fewer sick days
- 76 percent more engagement
- 29 percent more satisfaction with their lives
- 40 percent less burnout
- 50 percent greater likelihood of staying with the company

Trust isn't just having confidence that nobody is going to steal the stapler, says Zak. Trust is having confidence that people are going to behave like responsible adults—to be good, honest, and reliable. As a leader, you can do specific things to increase trust:

- Recognize excellence.
- Assign difficult but achievable goals.
- Give people discretion in how they do their work.
- Let people play to their strengths.
- Share information broadly.
- Build relationships intentionally.
- Facilitate the growth of the whole person and show vulnerability.

All those behaviors stimulate oxytocin production and generate trust.

Build Engagement by Being Engaged

Maybe you're not a people person. Maybe you worry that engaging your team using the behaviors listed previously will make things worse. Not likely. Gallup ran an engagement study that revealed three things:

- When a leader is supportive and appreciative, they build trust, and team engagement remains at nearly 100 percent.

- When a leader criticizes their people, engagement drops by more than 20 percent.

- And here's the shocker: when a team leader ignores, overlooks, or dismisses a team member, engagement drops by nearly 40 percent.

Ignoring people has twice the negative impact of criticizing them. If that research tells you anything, it should tell you to find ways to engage. Look for things you genuinely appreciate in people and voice them. If you have to criticize, psychologists recommend a six-to-one ratio of praise to criticism. So, praise lavishly and criticize sparingly. Just don't avoid people.

One of the best ways to build relationships (and trust) is to listen. Good listening is a hallmark of good leaders.

Start simple. If you haven't done it already, learn the name of everyone on your team so you can say it with confidence. This may sound basic, but Dale Carnegie's 1936 book *How to Win Friends and Influence People*, which is still a bestseller, dedicates a whole chapter to this topic. People love to hear their name. They love that you, their leader, know them by name. Frankly, it pisses them off when you don't, as in the following three examples.

Kenisha still gets irritated when she talks about someone who made a joke of never getting her name right. Not a funny joke.

Keithe, who worked at a high-tech company, had a manager who insisted he never learned her name because he couldn't tell her apart from the two other women who worked on the team. Keithe had pink hair.

Coach Ellen gave up on learning players' names long ago. She points and calls, "You! Red sweatshirt . . .!" vaguely amused at her own brashness. Judging from their narrowed eyes, the players don't find it quite as amusing. No one complains, but no one works quite as hard in her drills, either.

Once you're confident using people's names, learn what they care about. What are their goals and aspirations at work? What do they value? What do they want to be valued for? Your aim is not to be intrusive. It's to understand who you've got on your team so you can align with their motivations and help them play to their strengths.

Listen Like You Mean It

One of the best ways to build relationships (and trust) is to listen. Good listening is a hallmark of good leaders. According to a study of more than eighteen thousand leaders by consulting firm Zenger Folkman, the more skillful the leader is at listening, the higher their marks for generating trust and building relationships.

Listening is a skill you can improve. Keep in mind, your default listening mode may be colored by thinking preferences:

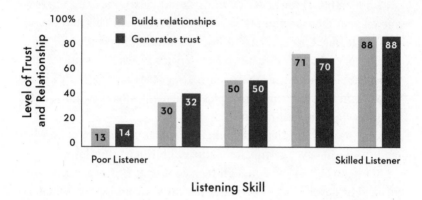

Impact of Listening Skills: The more skilled the listener, the more trust in the relationship.

People who like to clarify are often careful listeners. They like to gather information, and naturally show interest by asking questions. If you like to clarify, be sure your questions don't end up taking the conversation away from what needs to be said.

People who like to ideate are often open-minded listeners. They like to grasp the big picture, and naturally show interest by offering up ideas and connections. If you like to ideate, keep your own ideas in check until the other person has had a chance to fully express themselves.

People who like to develop are often earnest and sincere listeners. They like to improve situations, and naturally show interest by pointing out what could be done better. If you like to develop, be sure the person speaking has fully expressed themselves. When you do comment, point out what's positive about their approach before offering improvements.

People who like to implement are often attentive listeners. They like to get to the bottom line, and naturally show interest by pointing out what needs to be done. If you like to implement, hold that thought, and let the speaker share their experience before you suggest next steps.

Listening will help you learn more about the individuals on your team. It's a natural way to build relationships and a natural way to build trust at the same time.

Think of Trust in Layers

Start with the fundamentals and build from there.

Safety

At the foundation of trust is safety—physical, psychological, emotional, and financial. Trust dries up instantly in the face of bullying, harassment, or any kind of physical, psychological, or emotional threat. When pink slips start flying, or when people aren't making a living wage, it's tough to keep trust alive on a team. When people feel they have to cover their back (physically, emotionally, or financially), they will devote their energy to covering their back, not achieving your goals. If people feel unsafe on your team, do what you can to address that situation now. Toxic behavior can make a good team bad in a hurry. If it's out of your hands, seek help.

Clarity and Transparency

The next level of trust is clarity and transparency. Clarity builds trust. Vagueness weakens it. Dishonesty destroys it. Tools like the team charter can seed trust by setting clear expectations, agreements, and guidelines. As a leader, it's your job to establish these things early and communicate often with your team. When you don't know something, communicate that too. The best airline pilots give regular updates when their plane is stuck on the tarmac. It may not be their favorite part of their job, but they continue to communicate whether the news is good, is bad, or hasn't changed. It makes passengers comfortable to know that the pilot is in charge and being honest with them.

Belonging

At the next level of trust you find belonging. Humans are social animals. We are happiest in a group, but belonging is a process. It doesn't happen automatically when you assign people to a group or team. Belonging happens when people take on meaningful challenges together and move past the polite forming stage of a relationship, through the chaotic storming stage, and emerge on the other side. They are now part of a whole. They belong.

Respect

Respect is not just tolerating differences, it's valuing differences. Seeing people for who they are and valuing what they bring to the team motivates people to achieve and contribute. Diversity, equity, and inclusion work supports this layer of trust. So do thinking preferences. Apply your listening skills to understand individuals' goals and aspirations. All these contribute to help people bring their whole selves to work.

Psychological Safety

This is where teams reach their full potential. They harness their diverse thinkers, take on big challenges, and get outstanding results that none of them would have achieved working alone. Project Aristotle, Google's famous team study, identified psychological safety as the key characteristic of a high-performing team. As Amy C. Edmonson, leadership professor at Harvard Business School, explains, "Psychological safety is not about being nice—or about lowering performance standards. Quite the opposite: It's about recognizing that high performance requires the openness, flexibility, and interdependence that can develop only in a psychologically safe environment, especially when the situation is changing or complex."

Belonging happens when people take on **meaningful challenges together.**

Be the Leader People Want to Follow

Jeri was general manager for a $2 billion division of a Fortune 100 company. She ran the only division in the company that had posted double-digit growth, eight quarters in a row. Suffice it to say, Jeri ran a high-performing team. The team had a strategic planning session coming up, and they needed a facilitator. Two team members recommended Blair, so Jeri called him in for an interview.

"What's your approach?" she asked, skipping the niceties. "How would you lead us through this?"

Blair explained how he combined experiential activities and creative problem-solving techniques to tap people's best thinking.

"This is a team of highly professional people," she said. "We have a lot of work to do. We do not have time for any touchy-feely business."

"Sometimes that 'touchy-feely business' is exactly what you need to move things forward," Blair countered.

"I have no tolerance for that," she said. "I need someone to facilitate the work of the meeting."

Blair shrugged and thought to himself, on the spectrum of leadership, from task-focused to people-focused, Jeri was all task. His interview was apparently over, and she clearly wasn't going to hire him. But she did. Despite her skepticism, Jeri hired Blair to facilitate her high-stakes strategic planning meeting. She even agreed to let him do it his way. In preparation, Blair interviewed every member of her team. He braced for their complaints.

"She is the best manager of my career," one said.

"I would walk through a wall for this woman," said another.

To his surprise, story after story revealed the depth at which Jeri knew who they were, what they cared about, and what inspired them. One team member told a story of the night her mother went in for emergency surgery.

> I sat all night alone in the waiting room. At 6:00 a.m., the landline phone in the waiting room rang. With no cell coverage, it was the only way to reach people. It rang and rang. Then it stopped. Then it rang

again. The third time it started to ring, I picked it up. Somebody must be desperate, I thought, or have the wrong number. It was Jeri.

"How is your mother?"

"I don't know," I stammered. "They haven't given me an update."

"I've already talked with the team. Don't even think about coming in. We have you covered. All you need to do is take care of yourself and your mom. Call me if anything comes up. I will personally make sure it's taken care of. I'll call you later in the day to hear how your mom is."

Blair had Jeri all wrong. He couldn't wait to tell her. They kicked off the strategic planning session with a review of the group's FourSight Thinking Profiles. Jeri had a single preference to implement. On break, he took her aside and confessed, "You know, when we first met, you came off as a rather hard-nosed leader, but I've talked to everyone who works for you, and they would do anything for you."

Jeri looked Blair straight in the eye. She said, "How could I treat these people in any way other than with respect, caring, and openness? I spend more time with them than I do with my own family! As a leader, I'm only as good as my team. So, I try to lead a team everybody wants to be part of. That way, I get to pick from the best and brightest in the organization. We're almost guaranteed to succeed."

Jeri was tough. She had high standards. She expected great work and total dedication, but she earned it with equal work, caring, and dedication to her team. She had surrounded herself with top performers who knew they were seen by her, not just as professionals, but as whole people. Her team loved Jeri. They wanted to be like her. For many, working with Jeri was the high point of their career. "You don't have to be a perfect leader," she said. "Just be human. When you trust your people to be great, they almost always step up."

Whether she knew it or not, Jeri was manifesting the tenets of Edward Deci and Richard Ryan's research on motivation. People are motivated by challenges that help them achieve competence, connection with others, and some level of autonomy (a leader who trusts them to be great). Extrinsic motivators like money or position eventually fade in importance. But teams who are intrinsically motivated are unstoppable.

Jeri is living proof that a leader doesn't need to choose between task and relationship. The best leaders engender deep and abiding trust by choosing both.

ARE YOU more like Jeri or Shyla? Consider what you've learned about how leaders can build trust. Do you recognize excellence? Assign difficult but achievable goals? Give people discretion in how they do their work? Let people play to their strengths? Share information broadly? Build relationships intentionally? Facilitate the growth of the whole person? Show vulnerability? Acknowledge and appreciate people? Those are all the right moves.

In addition to trusting you, people also need to trust each other. Keep reading to understand how to foster trust among teammates and help ease the growing pains as your team develops.

• •

ACTIVITY
Trust in Me

• •

ON A PIECE of paper, make three columns, and label them "Start," "Stop," and "Continue."

- In the first column, thinking about trust, write a list of things you should start doing.

- In the second column, write a list of things you should stop doing.

- In the third column, write a list of things you should continue doing.

  Now, follow your own advice.

7

Speed the Path to High Performance

L ENA'S TEAM had a trust problem. A year ago, they were outper-
forming every similar team in their health insurance company.
Then corporate merged them with another high-performing
team. Some people lost jobs. Others took demotions. No one
was happy. The work was still getting done, but productive collaboration had been replaced by gossip and backbiting. Everyone had a
complaint about someone.

She acts like a bully.

He's way too cautious.

They're always pushing us forward.

She's always dragging us backwards.

It didn't help that the team was fully remote. The easy social bonds
of an office environment might have smoothed the rough transition.
But seven months had passed, and things were only getting worse.

Lena was nervous about the team's first in-person, week-long meeting. At the recommendation of a friend, she decided to open the week
with a FourSight workshop, hoping it would improve collaboration.
Her friend had told her to ask for me. While I still devoted most of
my time to running the company, I'd begun to deliver FourSight to
strengthen other teams. I knew it worked. I'd used it to strengthen
my own team.

I flew to Oklahoma City to deliver the workshop and met Lena for dinner the night before to get a briefing. "These are all good people," she told me. "They're dedicated to their work, and they're good at it. But they're not collaborating well, and it makes the work harder than it ought to be." She shook her head. "It's hard to see a team that was so compatible become overrun by cliques and conflict. Rumor has it someone has already applied for a transfer." She confided, "Some days I think they spend more time complaining to their cliques than actually doing the work."

"It sounds like your team is going through a storming phase," I said. "It happens on every new team."

"But this isn't a new team. We are all experts in this work, and we've all been on teams together before."

I explained, "As soon as the merger happened, your two teams became a brand new team. Most leaders hope they can integrate new people into a team without affecting performance, but adding or subtracting any team member sends the team back to the beginning of the team development cycle. You can resist it or ignore it, but it will still happen. The best you can do is speed up the cycle."

Team Development 101

Psychologist Bruce Tuckman, who studied the subject in the mid-1960s, identified distinct stages of team development. He labeled them: forming, storming, norming, and performing. Later scholars added two additional stages (re-forming and closure). Here's how each stage unfolds.

Forming

This initial stage happens when people first come together to form a team. This is the honeymoon stage, when everyone is on their best behavior, looking for commonalities, wanting to be included. People are optimistic about the team's prospects, but they are unsure and may be anxious about how it will work. They look to their leader for reassurance and guidance.

Storming

This is the tumultuous stage when people jockey for power and influence. They push back against leadership and test the boundaries. It's the team equivalent of adolescence. Personalities assert themselves. Work style differences surface. Egos emerge. Emotions flare. In the storming stage, teams figure out who's in charge and how things get done.

Norming

The calm that follows the storm. People find acceptable ways to interact. Power dynamics are sorted out. Lines of communication become clear. The team understands: Here's our purpose. Here's how we work together and make decisions in a healthy, sustainable way. It's negotiated. It's understood. It's explicit. People who can't abide by these terms can leave the team. Everyone else agrees to their roles, jobs, and purpose. They belong, and now they can get down to business.

Performing

This is when magic happens! The team now has purpose, trust, and a shared process to handle challenges. People know how to do their work and leverage one another's talents and differences. Collaboration thrives in a climate of psychological safety and productive debate. Team members may show up for the paycheck, but they stay late for the team. People push themselves to learn, improve, and achieve the team's goals.

Re-forming

Whenever someone leaves or joins the team, or the team recharters its purpose, re-forming occurs. This sends a team right back to the beginning of the team development cycle. Re-forming is hard on a team who shared the exhilaration of performing well together. At a

**Most leaders hope
to integrate new
people without affecting
performance,** but the
team still ends up going
back to the beginning
of the development cycle.

visceral level, people don't want to start over. They often have a sense of grief, loss, or frustration at losing what they've struggled to achieve. The good news is that seasoned team members can help speed the new team through the initial stages of the process so they can get back to performing sooner.

Closure

In this final stage of team development, the work of the team is done, and team members are ready to go their separate ways. This is an opportunity to celebrate accomplishments and close out the business of the team.

PRESENTED WITH such a tidy model, you may be tempted to think that all teams naturally progress through all the stages until they get to performing. Unfortunately, not all teams progress. Some teams get stuck.

Stuck in forming? Team members remain polite and avoid anything that could lead to conflict.

Stuck in storming? The conflict is palpable. The workplace is fraught with tension, resistance, suspicion, and gossip, and subterfuge is in the air. Role confusion and turf battles make people oppositional and reactive.

Stuck in norming? The team is functional but still not reaching its full potential.

Lena's team was stuck in storming.

"There is no way to avoid the storming stage," I told Lena. "Even good people sometimes behave badly at this stage."

I had met a handful of Lena's team members on a pre-meeting call. Beyond the growing pains of storming, their frustration seemed to center on one or two people who constantly seemed to ruffle feathers. And I recognized shades of thinking preferences in the language they used to describe their "difficult" teammates.

"I think this workshop may help your team get through the storming stage," I told Lena. I hoped I was right.

Trust and Thinking Preferences

That night, I thought back to a conversation with team-building expert Doug Reid. I had asked him to explain the relationship between trust and thinking preferences. "There's more than one kind of trust," Doug had explained. "I may trust you to take care of my kid, but when we're working on a problem together, I may not trust your approach. I may think you're doing it the wrong way. That lack of confidence can make it hard for us to work together, and it often traces directly back to thinking preferences."

Doug was describing a breakdown of trust that can happen when team members don't understand thinking preferences. They often mistake them for personality flaws and end up mistrusting those teammates who don't share their thinking preferences. They don't trust the way they go about solving challenges.

Research conducted by creative leadership adviser Ashley Goodwin, PhD, explored how thinking preferences affect people's confidence in others. She found that people who share thinking preferences often prefer to work with each other. More specifically:

- Clarifiers want to work with Clarifiers (and also Developers).

- Developers want to work with Developers (and also Clarifiers).

- Implementers only want to work with other Implementers.

- Ideators want to work with everybody, but not everybody wants to work with Ideators.

Pause here for a second and consider the implications.

That means, if you have a cognitively diverse team—which is a good thing—the odds of their wanting to work together are low—which is a bad thing. Remember the admonition of John Sedgwick? He's the psychologist who explained that people can sniff out differences instantly, and in the absence of positive labels, they will automatically assign negative ones. Goodwin's research proved his point. As humans, we have implicit bias against people with different thinking preferences.

We routinely assign negative labels to the very people who might help us solve problems more effectively.

"Difficult" People

On the morning of the workshop for Lena's team, we all met in the hotel lobby. People were cheery, friendly, prompt, and ready to work. No evidence of storming. These were polite, well-behaved professionals. Most of them were trained nurses whose current job was to review patient requests for medical procedures. They clarified on a case-by-case basis whether patients should be approved for care. Their work demanded a lot of clarifying. Not surprisingly, almost everyone on the team had a preference to clarify. In fact, the only two people with a *low* preference to clarify were the two "difficult" people on the team. They stuck out like sore thumbs.

"I have three goals for this workshop," I began. "To help you understand yourself, to help you understand each other, and to give you a common language to solve challenges together." I secretly had a fourth goal for myself: to help them better understand the "difficult" people on their team.

I began to explain the FourSight theory. "To solve a problem, you need four types of thinking. Most of us prefer just one. We like to work with people who share our thinking preferences, and we tend to avoid the people who don't, even though those are often the very people who could help us get better solutions."

The audience listened attentively. They were comfortable taking in research-based data like this. The clarifying energy on this team was so dominant, they had stopped seeing it as *one* way of thinking; it had become *the* way of thinking. My plan was to use this workshop to nudge everyone out of their cognitive comfort zones and help them see the value of other types of thinking.

In our first activity, I split the team into four groups. They didn't know it, but they were grouped by thinking preference. One group liked to clarify, one liked to ideate, one liked to develop, and one liked to implement. Each group was sent to a separate breakout room with a small box and told to take ten minutes to complete the challenge. The directions were hidden in the box. That got exactly the reaction I'd anticipated from the clarify group. They freaked out when they couldn't find them. They couldn't move forward without directions. One woman in the clarify group raised her voice when I went to check on the progress in her breakout room. "There are no directions!" she said accusingly. "Why would you give us an activity with NO directions?!" With a little nudging, she found the hidden directions, and like magic, she snapped back to her well-mannered self. She immediately sat down with her team to work through the challenge.

After ten minutes, we all reconvened in the conference room to debrief. "Who felt stressed to be doing something without clear instructions?" I asked.

All hands in the clarify group went up.

"Anyone else stressed about that?"

Not really.

"People who like to clarify like to have directions—in activities and in life. They like to get all the data first. They want to understand every aspect of the challenge before they start. They want directions to be sure they're going in the *right* direction. Conversely, when situations are ambiguous, they can suffer from analysis paralysis," I said.

"Now, let's talk about people who like to ideate. They like to see the big picture, make new connections, and come up with new approaches. Anyone here prefer to ideate?"

Only one person raised her hand. Tyra was head of research. She was one of the "difficult" people, the person who kept pulling the team backwards.

"Am I really the only person on the team with a preference to ideate?" Tyra asked, looking around in disbelief. Her teammates' eyes flashed in recognition. Maybe this was at the root of her difficult behavior.

"Sometimes people who like to ideate have trouble shutting off the idea faucet," I said. "Like you, I have a strong preference to ideate. I keep coming up with ideas even when the team has moved past the ideate stage. It can be hard on my team."

"Oh, I think I do that too," Tyra said.

Sometimes, the people
we label as "difficult"
**are the very people
who might help
us solve problems
more effectively.**

Heads nodded almost imperceptibly around the room.

"Is that hard for you guys when I do that?" Tyra asked her team-mates earnestly.

Heads nodded vigorously this time. People on the team who pre-ferred to develop chimed in: "We need time to get the solution just right. That's why your ideas are so frustrating," one said. "Just as we're closing in on the perfect solution, we have to pull back and start over from scratch. It requires a ton of rework," said another.

Tyra was stunned. "Really? I had no idea."

I reassured Tyra. "Your ideas are your gift. You're never going to stop having them, but you can change the way you communicate them. On my own team, I've learned to say, 'This is just an idea, so we don't have to do it, but can I share it with you?' It gives people the ability to hear what I'm saying as an idea, not as an assignment."

Tyra looked at the team. "Would that work for you?" More head nods. "I'm happy to work on that," she said.

People smiled in appreciation. Maybe she wasn't so difficult after all. Maybe her constant idea flow wasn't a personality flaw they were stuck with; it was a problem-solving style they could negotiate with.

One down, one to go.

The other "difficult" person on the team was Libby. People had described her as a bully. She had a single preference to implement. "People who like to implement are persistent, decisive, determined, and assertive," I read aloud from the research. Then I looked around the conference table. "That can feel a little pushy to people who like to clarify and take time to think things through."

People returned smug, knowing looks. Libby stuck out her chin in defiance.

"I don't know if you all noticed," I continued, "but this morning, when we all came into this room, I couldn't make the tech work. Libby immediately asked, 'What can I do?' She came right over and stayed with me until we had a solution. Nobody else even looked up. You were all following the directions, waiting patiently for me to start my pre-sentation. But Libby saw what needed to be done. She recognized we might be stuck, and she jumped into action. That's what people who prefer to implement do. They want things to move forward. They go after anything that might prevent the team from reaching its goals."

I looked at Libby, silently giving her the floor.

After a moment of silence, she spoke. "People have called me a bully," she said, showing the hurt. "I'm not a bully. I just like to get things done. Sometimes this group needs a push to get started."

All the people who liked to clarify looked at Libby as if they were seeing her for the first time. She looked down at her lap, not sure what to do with the attention.

"I get it now," said one teammate. "Sometimes, we get analysis paralysis. You're just trying to make sure we keep moving forward." Libby looked up, her smile on full beam. They could see her now. They could see that she was working to make the team better and contributing an energy the rest of them lacked.

When the team returned to the room after break, instead of sitting apart from each other in their executive swivel chairs, they piled around Lena, sitting on the edge of the table, pulling up chairs, leaning in, and quizzing each other.

"So, does it bug you when I do this?" asked one person.

"Oh, yeah," they replied. "That drives everyone bananas." (Laughter.)

I put down my slide clicker and smiled. There was no need to finish my slideshow. The language of thinking preferences had helped Lena's team build trust and psychological safety, and move through storming toward the next stage of the team development cycle.

There was more work to do—there always is—but for today, our work was done.

Accelerating the Cycle

Patrick Duhoux was the first to articulate how FourSight could become a deliberate method of accelerating the team development cycle. As pedagogical director of Dodeca, a Paris-based organizational development company, Patrick has served hundreds of teams throughout Europe.

A team stuck in storming will **never reach its full potential.**

He identified the particular boost that FourSight can give a team as they move through the team development cycle:

- A common language for problem solving speeds up the **forming** stage.

- A shared understanding of thinking preferences speeds up the **storming** stage, helping team members decipher interpersonal conflicts in an objective way.

- Problem-solving tools speed up the **norming** stage by helping teams perform effectively, even in areas of low preference.

- Finally, the combination of self-awareness and process-awareness helps teams succeed in the **performing** stage by equipping them to solve challenges quickly and effectively.

When you're a leader, in addition to helping your team understand thinking preferences, there are specific things you can do to accelerate the cycle of team development.

In forming, people are looking to you for direction. Use this time to

- draft a team charter;

- state the team's purpose;

- explain why each member has been chosen to be part of the team;

- assign roles and tasks;

- understand people's thinking preferences;

- share your strengths and weaknesses as a leader;

- be clear about your expectations; and

- establish some suggestions for working together (more about this in the next chapter).

In storming, it's easy to get frustrated with your team.

- Be patient.

- Don't take it personally.

- Gently point to the agreements you made in the forming stage.

- Ask each person if they can genuinely stand by these agreements.

In norming, the people on your team are finally committed to the team's success.

- Focus on developing the capabilities of each team member.

- Establish standard operating procedures.

- Help people recognize differences as potential strengths.

- Foster ways for people to be interdependent.

In performing, your role changes from manager to facilitator.

- Delegate more responsibility.

- Expect greater output.

- Assign tougher challenges.

- Facilitate communication.

- Celebrate progress.

- Focus on strategy.

In re-forming, although you may feel reluctant to start over, doing this step well will speed up the team development cycle.

- Restate the purpose of the team.

- Remind people of the team's goals, deliverables, timelines, standards, and expectations.

- Reinforce the team culture.

- Teach new team members how to engage.

- Let others go through the ritual of reengagement too.

In closure, honor what's been accomplished.

- Acknowledge people.

- Celebrate accomplishments.

- Close down the work of the team.

Teams go through a predictable cycle of development. As they progress, their level of effectiveness changes just as predictably. According to Tuckman's model, they start in the forming stage and progress through storming and norming before they get to performing. However, if they gain or lose members, they have to re-form and start all over again.

Although Tuckman's model gives the impression that all teams progress through the whole cycle, in actuality, some teams get stuck. A team stuck in storming will never reach its full potential.

NOW YOU can spot where you are in the team development cycle. You even know some ways to speed it up. What else can you do to intervene when a good team goes bad? Or when a bad team just doesn't seem to be getting better? That's what you'll learn in the next chapter.

GOOD PROGRESS

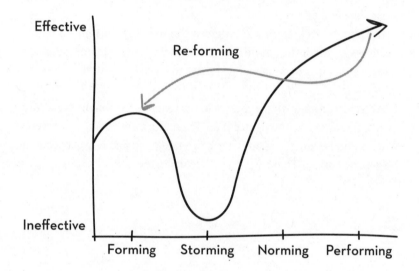

BAD PROGRESS

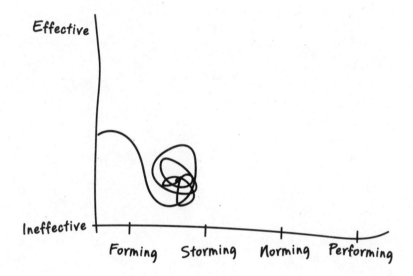

8

Create a Climate for Teams to Thrive

ARLY IN his career, when Blair was running ropes courses and trust falls, he needed a quick way to give people confidence that they could trust their teammates. After all, he was asking teammates to take physical risks together, and "trust" would be the difference between a trust fall and just a fall.

As soon as the team gathered, he would hand out a sheet titled "Suggestions for Working Together." It was a list of behaviors like *Express yourself. Listen generously. Look for what's possible.* He gave people a few minutes to look it over, make edits, and reach consensus on how they wanted to work together during the workshop.

"The beauty of this handout is its simplicity," Blair says. "They're not commandments. They're not commitments. They're just suggestions. Each one is observable and actionable. It doesn't describe a character trait. It's a behavior. It's something you can start doing, stop doing, and resume doing. And leaders can model the way." Without any formal decree about trusting one another, Blair had begun to establish a positive team climate.

Every fall, I do my own version of the "Suggestions for Working Together" exercise with the JV field hockey team I coach at our local high school. I gather my players in a circle and ask them: How do you want our team to work together? How do you individually want to show up? How should we treat each other? I write down their suggestions, and we all agree to honor them. As a group, we've just described our version of being a good team. So, when things go off track, as things always do, our suggestions can be our North Star and guide us back.

The Worst Team in the League

I love coaching sports teams. They share many of the same dynamics as organizational teams. When I was in high school, I played on a championship field hockey team. Field hockey was where I learned to be fierce, play hard, and work as part of a team. I wanted other girls to have that experience, so I helped launch a program at our local high school, and I volunteered as an assistant coach.

My knowledge of the game turned out to be woefully outdated. Now, we play on turf, a faster, more technical game. I had no idea how to coach it. The girls had fun, but we lost nearly every game. At the season's end, we ranked last in the league.

The next year, we held our record—last again.

Then we hired a bona fide field hockey coach. I was thrilled. Our team had a culture of camaraderie and good sportsmanship. Now we might even win a few games.

Aziz, our new head coach, was a tall, balding, athletic man with twinkling eyes, a handlebar mustache, and a penchant for banana-yellow golf shirts. Fifty girls tried out for field hockey that fall. Twelve of them were freshmen who had played on Aziz's middle school travel team. They had lightning stickwork. Many of them would make varsity. Aziz's eyes lit up when those freshmen flocked around him. He was devoted to his players, or at least those twelve. Other girls didn't seem to hold his attention quite so much. He confided to me that he had a secret agenda for the team: to shepherd those freshmen to a state championship when they were seniors.

He needed to find a way to keep those girls together. So, instead of tryouts, he assigned teams by grade: juniors and seniors would play varsity. Sophomores would play on the JV team. All his freshmen could play together on the freshman team. They would win every game, he said. It would be the beginning of their ascendancy.

Everyone was mystified. Why were top players stuck on the freshman team? Parents called in to complain. Aziz ignored them. Instead, he bought flashy new uniforms and made plans to travel to a tournament in St. Louis.

Why St. Louis? I wondered. *Are the teams there worse?*

The girls had more practical concerns. "Coach, the tournament is on Labor Day weekend," our captains pointed out. "People have plans."

"You're right," Aziz conceded. "We shouldn't go."

Ten minutes later, he gathered the whole team together and announced, "We're going to St. Louis!"

The captains were speechless.

Parents were not so speechless. The phone rang off the hook at the athletic department. How did this St. Louis tournament get on the schedule? Who would chaperone? Who would play? How much would it cost? Finally, Jack, the athletic director, put his foot down. The tournament was off.

Aziz went into a funk. His practices became disorganized. Girls stood around waiting for instruction. His funk grew worse every time he watched our beautifully clad players lose a game, which happened reliably twice a week. Emails filled Aziz's inbox with messages from upset parents and an increasingly grumpy athletic director.

A week later, I got a call from Jack. "I have some bad news for you. Aziz just quit."

"What?!"

"I'm calling to see if you'll take over as head coach."

"Me?"

"Well," he admitted, "I called around to see if any professional coaches could do it, but no one was available. Plus, I think the girls trust you. The parents trust you. If you're up for it, I'd prefer that you be the head coach for the rest of the season."

I didn't see that coming. I'd carved out a tidy role as the *assistant* coach, the one who boosted morale and remembered the Band-Aids, so girls didn't bleed all over their nice new uniforms. Head coach? Hardly. Still, I couldn't stand back and watch this program fail.

"I'll do it," I said.

Leaders are responsible for up to 67 percent of the team climate. That means you have the power to change what's happening significantly and quickly.

The next afternoon, Jack came to practice and made the announcement. Aziz had left. Coach Thurber would be the new head coach. Polite applause broke out among the players, but I could see the girls looking wide-eyed at each other.

I stepped forward. "Okay, guys, this is an unexpected turn of events. We need to figure it out together. I'll be counting on you a lot this season. There's no way I can do this without everybody's help. Coach Brody will be our technical coach. Varsity captains will be taking on new responsibilities. We'll also pick JV captains, who can help out. We'll be fine. For now, let's practice."

In a few days, we got our new routine down. Captains took charge of warm-ups. Coach Brody, a former player for the Jamaican national team, ran challenging drills. I took over the program, and my purpose was crystal clear: I wanted every girl to have a good team experience. To achieve that, I had to improve our team climate.

YOU OFTEN HEAR people bandy about the terms "climate" and "culture" as if they mean the same thing. They don't. Culture is the deeply rooted set of values that manifest into every aspect of the organization's character. Culture doesn't change quickly. Climate, on the other hand, is a snapshot of the team experience at any given time. Climate changes like the weather.

I was leading a team with a strong culture but a terrible climate. I needed help fixing it. For inspiration, I looked to the climate expert.

Swedish researcher Göran Ekvall identified ten dimensions that affect team climate. Nine make it better. One makes it worse. Unlike culture, where a team leader can hardly make a dent, climate is a place where leaders can have a big impact. Blair often asked leaders to evaluate their team climate by looking at the ten dimensions. Where were they strongest? What needed the most attention? What actions they could take to improve things?

I decided to use the same approach.

According to Ekvall, leaders are responsible for up to 67 percent of the team climate. That meant, as a team leader, I had the power to change what was happening significantly and quickly. So do you. So read carefully.

The Ten Dimensions
That Affect Team Climate

1 **Challenge and Involvement:** People find the work challenging—hard but doable. They are involved in helping shape the daily operations and long-term goals of the organization. People find joy and meaning in their work.

2 **Dynamism and Liveliness:** The atmosphere is filled with positive energy. Work is dynamic, and people are energized by new events, novel approaches, and different ways of thinking.

3 **Playfulness and Humor:** People are at ease. Conversations are peppered with humor, laughter, and spontaneity.

4 **Freedom:** People have some autonomy over how their work gets done. With more discretion over their day-to-day activities, they take initiative to acquire and share information.

5 **Risk-Taking:** People move forward in the face of uncertainty and ambiguity. They can put their big ideas forward and undertake bold initiatives even when the outcome is unknown.

6 **Idea Time:** People have time to think creatively—to test hunches or hypotheses and elaborate on new ideas, even those that are outside the original task or plan.

7 **Idea Support:** New ideas are treated with curiosity and interest. Management listens to proposals. Coworkers try out new ideas in a constructive atmosphere.

8 **Trust and Openness:** People feel safe at work and in their work relationships. Communication is open and straightforward. Initiatives go forward without fear of ridicule or reprisal in case of failure.

9 **Debate:** People actively put forward different views, ideas, experience, and knowledge. Many voices are heard. People challenge assumptions, opinions, ideas, and the status quo.

While the first nine dimensions support a productive climate, the tenth one destroys it.

10 **Conflict:** This is when emotional tensions are palpable. Individuals or groups dislike or hate one another. The atmosphere is one of warfare. Plotting, trapping, gossiping, and backstabbing are common.

Did you notice that "debate" and "conflict" are on opposite sides of the list? Ekvall found that debate is an asset. Conflict is a liability. Debate happens when you fight over an idea or issue. The goal is to achieve a better solution. Debate can get passionate, but afterwards, you go out for pizza. In conflict, the fight gets personal. People attack each other's identity, not just their ideas. Conflict hurts. Afterwards, you don't want to go out for pizza. You want to go out for revenge.

I WONDERED if Ekvall's list could help me turn a field hockey team around. I knew I didn't need to address all ten dimensions at once. I just needed to focus on two or three pain points. For me, those were obvious: challenge, trust, and conflict.

Some of my best players weren't being challenged because they had been assigned to the wrong team. Coach Brody and I worked together to rebalance the teams until the level of play suited the level of player.

Aziz had broken trust with players and parents. To begin to restore that trust, I wrote weekly email updates to parents and took time at practice to share information with players and answer their questions.

The conflict, which had been palpable between Aziz and the parents and administrators, began to dissipate. Instead of us working against each other, parents, administrators, and coaches were working together to make a good team experience for the girls.

By the season's end, the team climate was positive, but our game record was dismal. Once again, we ranked at the bottom of the league.

We had one game left—a playoff game to see which of the lowest-ranking teams would qualify for the post-season tournament. As the twentieth-ranked team, we were slated to play the thirteenth ranked, Saint Ignatius, giving them the benefit of an easy win.

Through it all, our captains had kept humor and dynamism alive. Coach Brody had sharpened everyone's skills and demanded their best. Hockey was fun again. We had two weeks left before the playoff game. As a team, we decided to go for it. We would draw up a brand-new team roster, pulling players from every class. We'd practice every day. We'd give it our all, rankings be damned.

On a sunny Saturday in mid-October, we drove to the beautiful Saint Ignatius campus in Chicago. As we walked into the stadium, we could see the barbecues, picnic tables, and congratulatory banners set up in anticipation of the big celebration. When you play the worst team in the league, you can count on a party after.

Our girls were anxious. Some had never played at the varsity level. The game began, and after a few nervous bobbles, the two teams seemed surprisingly well matched. Then, one team began to dominate. It was our team. When the final whistle blew, we had won the game 2–1. The girls went wild, hugging, high-fiving, taking selfies. We surged across the field to meet our cheering fans. I caught sight of the empty picnic tables and listless party banners. For a moment, I felt bad— but only for a moment. Our varsity team had won. We'd beaten the thirteenth-ranked team in our league. Nobody thought it was possible.

Actually, that's not true. We thought it *was* possible.

How did that happen? How did the worst team in the league, a team that lost its head coach mid-season, beat a team so much higher up the ranks?

We didn't win because we had better players. We didn't win because we had better coaches. We won because we had a better team. We'd improved our process of skilling up players, we had restored a positive team climate, and, best of all, we'd achieved our team purpose: to give every girl a good team experience.

None of that happened by accident or by luck. It happened because, while I still don't know enough about the technical aspects of field hockey, I finally had the skill set to lead a good team.

Most of us start with the wrong assumptions. We assume that good people lead good teams, and bad people lead bad teams. But Aziz was a good person and a talented coach who made a lot of errors and ended up with a team full of people problems. He had played favorites, hidden the team purpose from others, and let conflict fester. The team had gotten stuck in a permanent state of storming.

It's encouraging to know that a leader like you or me can turn a team like that around by attending to the right things. "A team climate is going to happen whether you attend to it or not," says creativity and innovation expert Marysia Czarski. "So be mindful of it, be alert, be present, and then generate it." When Marysia works with teams, she uses Ekvall's insights to help leaders identify their team's strengths and zero in on a few climate dimensions they could improve.

AS A LEADER, there are hundreds of things you can do to raise a healthy team. Not all will have an equal impact. Part Two of this book has been aimed at helping you narrow your focus. Now you know the importance of sharing your team purpose, earning people's trust, helping your team navigate smoothly through the team development cycle, and fostering a climate of productivity in which everyone on the team can thrive. Kudos to you. You know yourself better. You know your team better. Now it's time to get to know the challenges better.

. . . .

ACTIVITY
What Levers Will You Pull?

. . . .

CONSIDER EKVALL'S ten dimensions. As a leader, how are you doing on these dimensions? Do a quick sort.

- Which dimensions are strong for you and your team?
- Which ones really need attention?

Choose one of the dimensions that really needs attention and, with your team, come up with some simple, often no-cost or low-cost, things you could do to improve on that dimension.

Part Three

● ● ● ●

In the long history of humankind
(and animal kind, too) those who
learned to collaborate and improvise
most effectively have prevailed.

CHARLES DARWIN

KNOW YOUR CHALLENGE

•• 9 ••

Teams Need Challenges

EVERY MORNING, Blair and I have our happy routine. He gets a cup of coffee. I meditate. Then, we sit down with the *New York Times* Spelling Bee. Both of us are terrible spellers, I mean notoriously bad spellers. But we love the Spelling Bee. Why? Because it's just the right amount of hard—the perfect challenge.

According to the *New York Times*, tens of millions of people play their daily puzzles. What's the big attraction? Why beat your head against a word game when you could edify yourself with a simple "word-a-day" calendar?

Harvard professor Teresa Amabile found the best answer through her research. In her book *The Progress Principle*, she demonstrated that making progress, even a little progress, on hard goals makes people happy. The sense that they are moving and growing and progressing, and overcoming challenges and reaching goals, is gratifying. Making progress makes people feel grateful to be doing something worthwhile, to be part of something bigger, to be alive.

A challenge doesn't solve itself; it needs you to solve it. You can't be noncommittal, disengaged, or distracted. You have to get your hands in.

From Simple to Chaotic

Challenges often need a whole team to solve them. Here's the part most people miss: teams need challenges, too. In their book *The Wisdom of Teams*, Jon Katzenbach and Douglas Smith explain that teams and challenges have a symbiotic relationship. Challenges are the sort of puzzle that can bring a team together by bonding people to a common goal.

So why isn't everybody happy at work, where there are so many challenges? Because not all challenges are created equal. Let's explore the kinds of challenges that many of us have to face in work and life.

Simple Challenges

These challenges are fun. They keep you guessing but boost your confidence. There's a right answer, and you can guess it. They fall into the category of entertainment and team-building. They nudge you to the edge of your comfort zone but rarely push you beyond. The Spelling Bee is a simple challenge.

Complicated Challenges

These are doable but more demanding than simple challenges. They require you to step into the learning zone, and they take time and energy. Complicated challenges include editing code, onboarding staff, and planning your company retreat.

Complex Challenges

These types of challenges are daunting. They often have multiple layers, multiple players, multiple factors, and multiple solutions, and sometimes they require multiple teams. You're definitely in your learning zone here. If your talents rise to meet the challenge, you may experience a positive state of "flow." If the challenge proves too great, you may instead find yourself in a state of panic. Examples of complex challenges include starting a business, launching a new product line, inventing, and innovating.

Chaotic Challenges

These are sometimes called wicked challenges, and for good reason. They are huge, intractable, sometimes global, often threatening, always multisystem problems. Chaotic challenges like world hunger, poverty, war, injustice, and global warming can feel overwhelming, hopeless, even terrifying.

Challenges	Answerability	Process
Simple	There's a right answer.	Follow standard procedures.
Complicated	The answer is knowable.	Use critical judgment and experience.
Complex	Multiple answers are possible.	Use collaborative and creative problem solving.
Chaotic	Often unanswerable.	Seek patterns and solve subsets of the larger challenge.

According to leadership researcher Michael Mumford, the challenges you face will inevitably get harder as your level of leadership rises. Supervisors deal with simple challenges, enforcing regulations and following standard operating procedures. Managers deal with complicated challenges, applying their judgment and political savvy to forward the goals of the teams and the organization. Executives deal with complex challenges, finding ways to grow a business, fixing or transforming the status quo, and inspiring others to follow. World leaders deal with chaotic challenges, trying to solve the unsolvable—bless them.

Good leaders know how to harness their teams to help. For that, leaders and teams need the right tools, but you probably didn't get them in school. In elementary school, you could get a gold star for solving simple challenges—the ones with the answer in the back of the book. As you progressed, you learned to solve complicated

• • • •

Challenges can bring
a team together by
**bonding people to
a common goal.**

challenges—like writing a five-hundred-word essay or setting up a science lab. At first you may have struggled to wrap your head around these challenges, but your teacher had a firm grasp of how to guide you to the right outcome.

Complex problems aren't like that. There are no answers in the back of the book. There are no teachers to walk you through it. You're on your own, facing an ambiguous issue with multiple paths forward, some better than others, but none that guarantees a specific outcome. Now you're up against questions like, How do we turn this business around? How can we make a positive social impact? How do we prepare for the next disruptive threat?

Most of us never learned a language to solve problems like that, but, ready or not, that's what we're up against. Every five years, the World Economic Forum publishes the *Future of Jobs Report*, which lists the ten job skills essential for success in the coming years. The skills change slightly over time, but in the twenty-first century, problem solving of every variety dominates the list. Today's workplace requires critical thinking, creative thinking, and collaboration to solve complex problems.

This is the direct result of the dirty little secret no one ever mentions. Technology, our beacon of hope that would eliminate all the drudgery from our lives, has taken over the simple challenges and left us with the complex ones. Teams that once simply collected data are now expected to extract meaning from it. Teams that once hammered out work are now expected to innovate how the work gets done. And these days, it's not just executive leaders who get complex problems to solve, it's every leader.

Problem Solving Is a Universe

Given the increase in demand for complex problem solving, it's no surprise that a parade of problem-solving processes have made their debut in the business world. Different groups favor different ones. You may have heard of some of them: design thinking, Lean Six Sigma, agile, Google Design Sprint.

These processes are all smart ways to help people go from problem to solution. Each uses different language, stages, and tools to get the job done, but they share one unifying factor. (You're going to like this.) If you drill down, you find they are all powered by the same four types of thinking: clarify, ideate, develop, and implement.

Bingo! You just discovered why you spent all that time in Part One learning about the four types of thinking. Good news: they are the four types of thinking that power every problem-solving process under the sun. So, when you understand thinking preferences, you understand how people are going to engage in whatever process you throw at them.

Five Common Problem-Solving Methods

When our son came home from his first corporate job, he complained that the workplace was full of competing problem-solving processes. It was confusing for people, he said. "You guys should really publish an article and explain the differences." Blair and I were flattered that our son thought us capable of eliminating the confusion, but we do love a challenge. As a team leader, if you understand the difference between these methods, you won't get caught in the crosshairs of different teams using different problem-solving approaches. So, here's our attempt.

The following expert process models are tailor-made for the work they support. Before you adopt one, just be sure it's a fit for the work you do.

Design Thinking

Primary users: those designing a product or service

Desired outcome: a tested prototype of a product or service that truly meets a user need

Thinking skills: clarify + develop

Design thinking is a problem-solving process that puts the end user at the center of every stage. So, designers who want to build a better mousetrap don't just study mousetraps, they study homeowners trying to get rid of mice. They take time to observe the behaviors and frustrations of the people who will ultimately use the product or service they create in order to clarify what a better mousetrap truly needs to be. Then they come up with an idea, informed by customer data.

Before they mass-produce the idea, designers make a prototype and ask for user feedback to get it right. The process is iterative, not linear, and is centered on improving through feedback and data. Design thinking was popularized by the IDEO design company and the Stanford d.school, which have spread its teachings far beyond the design world. Today, people in all kinds of endeavors use design thinking to clarify customer needs and get customer feedback early and often in the problem-solving process.

Lean Six Sigma

Primary users: people in operations and process control

Desired outcome: system improvements that both reduce waste and increase quality

Thinking skills: clarify + develop

Lean Six Sigma is actually a mash-up of two different problem-solving processes (Lean and Six Sigma) that work together to improve quality, safety, and efficiency.

Lean focuses on eliminating waste and streamlining processes. Think of Henry Ford creating an assembly line to produce the Model T— same car, same color—in record time. He achieved maximum flow but no variety. Japanese engineers at Toyota figured out how to achieve both flow and variety. They are credited with the beginnings of modern Lean Manufacturing. These days, Lean is used to streamline all kinds of things, from loading cruise ships to staging emergency rooms for maximum efficiency.

Six Sigma, by contrast, focuses on reducing defects to improve over-all quality in the manufacturing process. The combined Lean Six Sigma approach removes statistically significant variations through process improvements and leads to greater efficiency and improved quality control. It makes small improvements that can add up to big wins.

Agile

Primary users: software developers and other product creators

Desired outcome: products that iterate to find their market fit

Thinking skills: develop + implement

Agile is a project management framework that is iterative in nature. Technically, it isn't a problem-solving process at all. It's a set of principles and values that help teams collaborate with a bias for action. Agile originated in the software development space, where innovators were frustrated at the painfully slow method of product rollout. The so-called waterfall method was so bogged down by documentation and planning that it neglected to check in with customers until after the product hit the market.

Agile, by contrast, is light on its feet. Scrum is the methodology agile incorporates to manage projects. Scrum encourages people to self-organize into teams overseen by a scrum master, who ensures that everything is running smoothly. Agile tries to bring Minimum Viable Products (MVPs) to market to help the product iterate, improve, and find its market fit.

Sprints

Primary users: teams launching new projects

Desired outcome: a working prototype to test with users

Thinking skills: ideate + develop

Sprints are time-boxed problem-solving exercises with a specific outcome in mind. They come in many shapes and sizes. The Google Design Sprint, described in Jake Knapp's bestselling book *Sprint: How to Solve Big Problems and Test New Ideas in Just Five Days,* is a five-day facilitated session that allows a team to bring a concept from idea to prototype, and even do customer testing. This type of sprint was pressure-tested by Google Ventures, the venture capital investment arm of Alphabet that works with tech companies in the growth stage. The sprint helped teams walk away with a validated idea for a product or service. Agile sprints are an entirely different animal. Agile sprints are used by scrum teams to tackle a small portion of a larger project. An agile sprint generally lasts between one and four weeks.

FourSight

Primary users: leaders, teams, and facilitators who solve complex problems

Desired outcome: an effective solution to a challenge that needs new thinking

Thinking skills: clarify + ideate + develop + implement

FourSight is a problem-solving system that equips people to think, connect, and solve problems more effectively. The process is simple: FourSight combines the four types of thinking necessary to solve a complex problem (clarify, ideate, develop, and implement) into a four-stage problem-solving process. "For team leaders who don't have a formal process, this can serve as your default," says Russ Schoen, FourSight partner and facilitation lead. "Your teams will be much better served than if you had no process at all." Then, unlike other problem-solving approaches, FourSight teaches people to understand their thinking preferences within the process so they can work together with less friction and solve challenges more effectively. Because it is versatile, easy to use, and nearly universal in its potential applications, some consider FourSight the Swiss Army knife of problem-solving processes. Russ uses it to help groups do strategic planning, new product development, brand planning, marketing, and other complex challenges that require collaboration and new thinking.

YOUR TEAM may already use one of these processes or have your own. Ideally, you're using a process model that's tailor-made for the type of problems you solve. If it's working, keep it up. But what happens when, like our son, you suddenly find yourself trying to collaborate with people who use different process models?

You May Need a Decoder Ring

Mike Ackerbauer, PhD, calls himself a "cognitive sherpa." It's an apt description. He guides teams who come together with different problem-solving processes through the treacherous terrain of collaboration. At IBM, where Mike is a senior business technology leader, he speaks fluent design thinking, agile, Lean Six Sigma, Google Design Sprint, and FourSight. If people who speak multiple languages are called polyglots, Mike is a process-glot.

Mike was the guy who brought FourSight to IBM. He uses the four types of thinking as his secret decoder ring. It's how he gets all those process models to connect. On a flowchart of any problem-solving process, Mike can pinpoint where clarify, ideate, develop, and implement happen. Those four types of thinking become a common language, not only showing how different problem-solving processes relate, but anticipating how people (and teams) will relate to the different stages of those problem-solving processes.

Mike says that design thinking emphasizes the front end of the problem-solving process. The intense focus on clarifying the end user's real need is the way to ensure you're solving the right problem. Design thinking has great clarify tools, including consumer interviews, focus groups, and ethnographic research. The whole approach puts the end user (not the designer) at the center of the problem-solving process. When you study the thinking preferences of designers, you can see why. As a group, designers don't much like to clarify. They like

• • • •

If you drill down, you find
problem-solving processes
are all powered by the same
four types of thinking:
**clarify, ideate, develop,
and implement.**

to ideate. Left to their own devices, they'll come up with an idea, fall in love with it, and design it—whether or not it meets an end-user need. Design thinking has built-in safety checks to ensure designers do the work to clarify and solve a problem the end user really has, so designers aren't blindsided by their own preference to ideate.

Agile, says Mike, emphasizes the back end of the problem-solving process. Agile has great strategies to implement. It was originally created to help software developers move products to market. The FourSight research shows that people in IT and software development have a thinking preference to develop (how apropos). They like to work out the perfect solution, and that takes time. The agile approach keeps them from languishing in the develop stage of the problem-solving process, because it is chock-full of implement tools and techniques that push work to completion.

When Mike brought FourSight into IBM, he got a lot of questions. (IBM is full of people who like to clarify.) Specifically, they asked, how is FourSight different from MBTI, StrengthsFinder, DISC, and the other assessments we already use? Those are personality assessments, he told them. They measure who you are. The FourSight Thinking Profile is a problem-solving assessment that measures how you like to think—especially when you approach problems that require collaboration and innovation. Personality assessments give you self-awareness. FourSight gives you both self-awareness and process-awareness, which helps teams solve tough challenges.

Mike introduced FourSight to Casimer DeCusatis, an IBM Distinguished Engineer and Master Inventor with over 150 patents to his name. DeCusatis was intrigued and wrote a journal article comparing several different ways to build and sustain cross-generational innovation teams. FourSight outranked other methods because its unique combination of self-awareness and process-awareness helped teams approach problems more effectively.

NOW YOU KNOW that all processes are not created equal. In the next chapter, we'll teach you the secret to making *any* process yield better outcomes.

. . . .

ACTIVITY
Analyze Your Team's Process

. . . .

WHAT PROBLEM-SOLVING PROCESS do you use on your team? Is it formal or explicit? If so, take a minute to determine where the four critical types of thinking (clarify, ideate, develop, and implement) show up. Does your process tend to prioritize one type of thinking over others?

·· 10 ··

The Secret to Better Solutions

THE SECRET to getting better solutions is to add creative thinking to your problem solving. You might say, "But I'm not creative!" About half the people in Blair's training programs say that. Don't let it stop you. Creative thinking is like a muscle: the more you use it, the stronger it gets. There are specific ways to strengthen your creative thinking. You'll learn some of them in this chapter. To start, a little history may prove useful.

Making the Creative Leap

In the 1950s, J.P. Guilford, president of the American Psychological Association, challenged his colleagues to broaden their study of psychology beyond mental dysfunction to investigate mental health—the branch we now call positive psychology. Guilford specifically urged his colleagues to research creativity. He wanted us to understand the mechanism that allows people to add creative thinking to problem solving.

Guilford himself joined the hunt. Creative thinking, he found, needs more breathing room than other kinds of thinking. Instead of following a logical, linear sequence, it pulses like a beating heart. Guilford described the pulsing movement with two verbs: "diverge" and "converge."

When you diverge, you expand your thinking and generate lots of options. Since new ideas often come from combining old ideas, you want to invite every idea to the party in hopes they will couple up and make promising new ideas. Only after you've generated dozens of options, do you converge. You consider all your options and choose the best, making sure some new thinking makes the cut.

Creative thinking also requires a psychologically safe space, so people can explore options and choose novelty. The following guidelines help create that space, whether you're thinking alone or with others.

When you diverge:

- Defer judgment. (Don't cut down people or ideas.)

- Strive for quantity. (Let all the options emerge.)

- Build on others. (Make new options by connecting old ones.)

- Go for wild, novel alternatives. (It's easier to tame a wild choice than energize a dull one.)

When you converge:

- Be affirmative in your judgment. (Look for what you like.)

- Check objectives. (Does the option fit the criteria for success?)

- Be deliberate. (If you rush, you're likely to pick the most familiar options.)

- Keep novelty alive. (Challenge yourself to bring new thinking forward.)

Does this look and sound like brainstorming to you? Well, it is—almost. Here's the crux of the issue. Most of us associate brainstorming with generating ideas, which only happens in the ideate stage. The person who coined the term "brainstorming" was a friend of Guilford's. His name was Alex Osborn and he was an ad man (the original

"O" in the advertising agency BBDO). Osborn was fascinated by the process his creative staff used to generate ideas.

When Guilford and Osborn brought their worlds together, they realized that diverging and converging happen at every stage. You have to diverge and converge when you clarify the challenge, ideate on possibilities, develop your solution, and implement it.

Why should you care? Because divergent thinking is essential to good leadership. This isn't conjecture. A team of creativity researchers studied military leaders and found that their ability to diverge was more predictive than their experience or intelligence in determining whether their followers would consider them good leaders. People want to follow the leader with the best solutions. The best solutions come from the best ideas, and the best ideas come from divergent thinking. Divergent thinking is a core leadership competency. It will help you get better solutions and more devoted followers. Plus, according to the researchers, it's a significant predictor of promotion to higher ranks.

That's why you care.

How Can You Get Better Solutions?

Try this out—first on your own, then in a pair, then in a group. The next time you have to make a decision, diverge on options before you converge on a choice. Make it part of the way you work. The process can look as simple as this.

I often collaborate with FourSight partner Greg Sonbuchner, our tech lead. In addition to studying computer science, Greg has also studied the science of creative thinking. He knows the value of diverging before you converge. Whenever we develop a new online feature for FourSight, Greg asks his IT team to mock up three or four options. At our meetings, we review the options, but rather than choose one, we keep diverging, asking ourselves, How can we make this better? What if we condense that graphic? Or eliminate it? Maybe we simplify the text? We throw out ideas and knock them around. At some point, my

• • • •

**The best solutions come
from the best ideas,**
and the best ideas come
from divergent thinking.

preference to implement rears its head. I get impatient. *Let's decide already!* But Greg likes to develop, and I've worked with Greg long enough to know that if I give him time to refine the options, the right one will emerge. It will stand out for both of us. Then there's no struggle. We invariably find a better solution. And everyone wins.

We've all been in bad problem-solving meetings. They generally go something like this: A problem comes up. You throw out an idea. Someone immediately criticizes the idea, and you find yourself defending it, even if you weren't particularly attached to it. The meeting becomes a verbal volley of attack and defend. Your idea either wins or loses. (You feel as though *you* either win or lose.)

There are three big problems with this approach. First, you've debated only *one* option, the first one that popped out of someone's mouth. Second, you've gotten egos involved and spent time defending ideas that aren't even that good; good ideas usually show up after the obvious ones and the bad ones are explored. Third, you've likely only heard from the loudest, brashest people in the room, the ones who love verbal sparring. The more analytical members of your team (i.e., the people who like to clarify and develop) usually withdraw when problem solving becomes a combat sport. That means you lose their valuable insights.

Good meetings work differently. A problem comes up. Someone phrases the problem as a question (more on that in the next chapter). Everyone in the group takes a few minutes to diverge on ideas, add and build on ideas, and make them better. Then the group converges on the best ones.

It takes about the same amount of time to run a good meeting as it does to run a bad one, but good meetings offer some distinct advantages. Everyone gets a chance to share their thinking, so the circle of decision-making is more inclusive. Buy-in is higher. The perspectives are broader. You spend most of your time talking about the good ideas, not the bad ones, and the solution is better because the best idea wins.

In case you needed proof: a large-scale study, conducted at the Center for Applied Imagination at Buffalo State University, found that groups trained to separate divergent and convergent thinking improved the quality and quantity of their output by a whopping

300 percent. Even untrained groups, who were simply instructed to diverge before they converged, got better results than groups left to their own devices.

Janice Francisco, a graduate of the Center for Applied Imagination, was training union members to collaborate with their employer to improve dangerous work conditions at a newly opened gold mine in northern Canada. "The job of these union members was not easy," said Janice. "They were not managers. They were skilled tradespeople, who suddenly found themselves managing complex problems, people, and personalities." To play that role more effectively, Janice taught them the FourSight Framework and gave them their thinking profiles. Then they got down to solving the problem at hand. One team reported, "We've achieved more in the last half hour using this process than we have in the last six months."

You can do this kind of problem solving on a small scale, the way Greg and I do, or you can do it on a larger scale to create a psychologically safe space that invites everyone to explore the options.

The Power of Inclusive Problem Solving

One February, Blair flew to Georgia to facilitate a two-day meeting in a small town three hours south of Atlanta. It was a business simplification project. The sponsor wanted to squeeze $14 million of costs out of the supply chain without cutting head count. Blair would use the four-stage FourSight Framework to do it.

Before the meeting, he gave the project team ten weeks to compile a comprehensive "fact book" that included every data point from sourcing, transport, manufacturing, and retail placement of the product. Plant workers caught wind of the effort and let their skepticism be known. "Be prepared," the plant manager warned Blair. "You may not get the warmest welcome from the workers at the site."

But when Blair arrived in Georgia, everything seemed in order. More than sixty people arrived for the two-day, in-person summit. They came from the local plant and every corner of the company, representing operations, purchasing, finance, logistics, and manufacturing. Their job was to comb through the fact book, clarify the right problems to solve, generate ideas, and develop solutions that, when implemented, would save millions.

Blair launched the event the way he always did. He clearly stated the purpose of the team that had gathered: we're here to identify cost-saving opportunities without compromising quality or jobs. He shared the "Suggestions for Working Together," and he introduced the four stages of the FourSight Framework. Those were all things he knew would help propel good thinking.

Then they got to work. They diverged and converged on challenges, ideas, and solutions. At the end of two days, when they added up the potential savings, they had identified $67 million, far exceeding their $14 million goal. Blair was relieved. The team had taken on a big challenge and solved it. Everyone, including the plant workers, had offered useful insights. The project sponsor was so pleased, he congratulated the group and sent everyone home early. People left with smiles on their faces.

Blair and his co-facilitators stayed in the room, taking down flip charts and wrapping things up. The plant manager came over to thank Blair and his facilitation team. Then he said something that caught Blair by surprise. "Look, I have absolutely no doubt that you've helped us hit our dollar target, but to me, here's what's really valuable. Do you see this room?" He turned and looked over his shoulder. "There are still people sitting around every single one of these tables. It's been forty minutes since you told everyone they could go home. I've worked at this company for thirty years. I can tell you, these guys checked out years ago," he said. "If you had told me, after two really hard days of using their brains, they would still be here, I wouldn't have believed you. But here they are, talking about work. Some of them don't even talk to each other anymore." He shook his head. "I really appreciate all the money you've helped us save. But I would have paid your entire fee just for this. You gave us our team back."

Blair felt proud. He was happy for his client, but he knew he didn't deserve all the credit. He had simply given people a common language and held a space for them to diverge and converge in each stage of the problem-solving process. As a result, the right problems got clarified. The best ideas emerged. The smartest solutions were developed, and the team was ready to implement action steps that could save them over four times their original goal.

When you take on big challenges with a hands-in, creative problem-solving process, you don't just end up with better solutions. You end up with better teams.

IN THE NEXT CHAPTER, we'll equip you with two power tools for problem solving with your team.

• •

ACTIVITY
Try Creative Problem Solving
on Your Next Challenge

• •

READY TO TAP INTO the power of divergent and convergent thinking to solve your own challenge? Use a free version of the FourSight Challenge Navigator (at foursightonline.com/challenge-navigator), which will walk you through the FourSight Framework. Bring a goal, wish, or challenge and leave with an action plan.

• • • •

When you take a
hands-in approach,
you don't just end up
with better solutions.
**You end up
with better teams.**

GOOD
PROBLEM SOLVING

BAD
PROBLEM SOLVING

•• 11 ••

Power Tools for Problem Solving

USING THE FourSight Framework for creative problem solving sounds like a great way to face a challenge. But what if I get stuck?

I have one word for you: *tools*. Tools make difficult jobs easier. There are dozens of problem-solving tools to help you clarify, ideate, develop, and implement. They come with step-by-step instructions and often lead to breakthrough solutions. But there's no need to memorize an entire tool library. In this chapter, you'll learn the two tools that leaders who took Blair's creative problem-solving courses say they use the most. Both work like a charm, even for beginners.

Tool #1: Phrase Challenges as Questions

Deanie started her job at one of the world's largest food and beverage companies with loads of confidence. She was smart and talented, and had already moved up from associate to senior brand manager. Rumor had it, her name might soon be thrown in the ring for director.

But lately, Deanie had trouble keeping up. Her promotions came with an expanding list of responsibilities, and she didn't see how she could work any harder or dig any deeper. She looked at people higher up in the organization. How were they doing it? she wondered. They just must be made out of different stuff.

To add to her crushing workload, her manager had booked her into a two-day course on creative problem solving. What the heck? She had real work to do. She had no time for this! But Deanie went. She was surprised that the instructor, Blair, taught such practical approaches to problem solving. They seemed almost obvious once you knew them. She could easily incorporate this into her work.

Blair taught her to generate lots of options (a.k.a. diverge) before she made her top choice (a.k.a. converge). She learned to clarify, ideate, develop, and implement, and to use tools to improve her performance in each stage. The tool that stuck most with Deanie was "Phrase Challenges as Questions."

It's a clarifying tool, and the premise is simple. You take your problem, challenge, or chronic complaint and phrase it as an open-ended question.

Instead of stating it as a fact, like this: *I can't keep up with all this work!*—you turn it into an open-ended question, like this: *How might I manage my growing workload?*

That simple shift makes a big difference. Brains are remarkably suggestible. When you tell yourself, *I can't keep up with all this work!* your brain obliges by cuing up emotions like stress, anxiety, and insecurity.

If, instead, you ask, *How might I manage my growing workload?* your brain will go to work looking for useful answers to your question. A challenge question effectively turns your problem into a brain teaser, and a puzzle for your brain to solve. The trick is to start your question with a phrase that invites new thinking. These four question starters all work well:

- How to...?
- How might...?
- In what ways might...?
- What might be all the...?

Maybe it sounds formulaic. You can't imagine yourself saying that. The trick here is to try it. After Blair's training, Deanie went back to work and tested out this new clarifying tool. She discovered two things: Phrasing challenges as questions helped her solve the right problem. It also engaged others to help find the solution.

One day, two members of Deanie's team approached to her desk with their "problem faces" on. She sensed trouble. The team had invested $100,000 to set up a product launch early in the new year. They had only $1,000 left in their year-end budget, and they still needed one more critical product sampling to happen on the west coast.

Looking defeated, the two assistant brand managers sat down in front of her.

"We have to push the product launch back," said one.

"We can't make the sampling happen before the end of the year," said the other.

"What's the problem?" Deanie asked.

"Our San Francisco agency wants $10,000 to run the sampling, and we don't have the budget."

Deanie understood the facts. The agency wanted $10,000. They didn't have $10,000. Poof. No sampling. No first-quarter launch.

Then she began to smile. "Let's step back for a minute," she said. "How might we make the sampling happen on time and with the budget we have?"

"We just told you. We can't do it," said one.

"We've got to figure out how to push the product launch back," said the other.

She tried again, posing the question a slightly different way. "In what ways might we make the sampling a reality?"

They stared back at her blankly. They had just told her it couldn't happen. Twice. The two assistant brand managers looked at each other and shrugged. Apparently, she was serious. Then one of them had a moment of recognition. "This isn't that creative problem-solving stuff you've been studying, is it?" he asked with skepticism.

"Well, this seems like an awfully good time to try it out," Deanie said.

"But the product launch is on the line."

"Exactly," she said.

To humor her, they began to throw out ideas.

Use our San Francisco–based salespeople.

Fly to San Francisco and do the sampling ourselves.

Hire a different agency.

Get part-time help.

• • • •

Phrasing challenges as questions helps you solve the right problem. It also engages others to help find the solution.

In minutes, the three of them had generated a dozen ideas. After diverging, they converged on a promising idea. Finding the solution took them less time than they had spent arguing why the problem couldn't be solved.

Before the year was out, they ran a successful sampling program that was on schedule and under budget, and the product launched without a hitch. Deanie's career continued to speed along on the fast track.

Soon after that, she was invited to attend the signing of a partnership agreement between her company and another billion-dollar company. Top executives, who had flown in from around the country, took their seats at the conference table. She was happy to be a fly on the wall at such a momentous occasion. The signing was mostly ceremonial, but suddenly egos started to bristle. In a merger of two equals, executives on both sides wanted to assert their dominance.

"There's a problem with the formatting of the contract," said one.

"That's how we do it," countered another.

These executives were supposed to close the deal, not fight about it, but tension continued to rise until it looked as though both sides were ready to walk.

From her seat along the back wall, Deanie stood up. She was the youngest person in the room and one of the only women. "Excuse me," she said. "How might we finish signing the deal first and fix the formatting later?" The entire roomful of executives swiveled to see who was asking. Her question broke the tension long enough for everyone to take a breath, refocus, and sign the document—which promptly went to the designer for reformatting.

Deanie couldn't wait to share the news with Blair.

"Now I get it!" she enthused. "I was watching this multimillion-dollar deal start to sink. The people at the table were smart, but they didn't have the moves to get things back on track. It's just a skill!" she said. "You either have it or you don't." Every time Deanie applied the skill, she saw the payoff. It's just what leadership researcher Michael Mumford would have predicted. He found that the higher you move up in the organization, the more often you are called upon to define problems, seek novelty, and navigate ambiguity. To lead, he concluded, you must master the skills of creative problem solving.

Deanie was a good student and continued to learn more moves. She rose to the C-suite at her company and went on to serve as president and CEO of two other companies. Years later, reflecting on her career success, she said, "Creative problem solving is one of the most critical skills for smart people taking on big problems."

You don't need to be headed for the C-suite to make this tool work for you. You may worry you'll sound awkward if you start to phrase challenges as questions. So, try it out on yourself first. Phrase your own challenges as questions. Then follow Deanie's example and try it out with others. The results may surprise you.

Tool #2: Praise First (POINt)

The second problem-solving tool leaders seem to love is Praise First, the POINt evaluation tool. It comes from the develop stage of the process, and it works to strengthen and improve ideas. It also happens to strengthen and improve relationships along the way.

Blair once taught Praise First in a two-day training in creative problem solving for a group of no-nonsense plant managers. These were operations people—the ones in charge of "making the stuff" that made money for the company. Let's just say that their patience for fruity creative fluff was paper-thin.

At the end of the first day, Blair assigned homework. They had to use Praise First and make a POINt evaluation on someone's idea before class the next morning.

"POINt" stands for Pluses, Opportunities, Issues, and New thinking. The tool disciplines you to see what's good about a new idea, before you get busy explaining why it couldn't possibly work.

Most ideas don't come out fully formed. And most of us, in an effort to be helpful, efficient, or proactive, react to new ideas by pointing out their flaws. In other words, when people float out a delicate new idea bubble, we put a pin to it. Ouch.

Instead of identifying the flaws in an idea, Praise First requires you to take the opposite approach. Praise the new idea first. To do that, you make a POINt evaluation. When someone offers a new idea, first articulate the following:

- **Pluses:** What's good about it? What are its positive features?

- **Opportunities:** What would be possible if the idea worked? Start with, "It might..."

- **Issues:** After celebrating its pluses and opportunities, you can raise your concerns. Phrase them as open-ended questions, using the same handy phrases listed in the previous tool: "How to...?" "How might...?" "In what ways might...?" or "What might be all the...?"

- **New thinking:** Now generate new ideas to address the issue.

Praise First is a valuable strategy to keep you from getting caught up in what's wrong with an idea and missing the pearl of opportunity that may be hidden. A POINt evaluation not only prevents you from closing down the potential brilliance of an idea, but it also signals to the other person that you genuinely see the value of their thinking. If they feel validated, they are more likely to listen to your concerns because they know your intent is to make their idea stronger.

Whenever Blair shares this new tool with leaders, their reaction is predictable: Well, *that* won't work.

This day was no different. When he assigned the POINt homework, he couldn't help but notice a few eye rolls in the back of the room. Bobbie, a plant manager and one of the eye rollers, was an ex-military officer with the demeanor of a drill sergeant. She had already announced to the class that she didn't see any value in this training. She had two jobs to do. The first was to make sure all her people were safe. The second was to make money for the company by producing the product in the most efficient way possible. When she finished job one, she focused on job two. When job two was done, she was back to job one. Creative problem solving? She didn't see the point. When the group broke for the day, Bobbie left without a backward glance. Blair sighed and folded up his laptop.

The next morning, Bobbie was one of the first to arrive. She took Blair aside and said, "I'd like to share my homework first." Blair agreed. You didn't disagree with Bobbie.

When class started, Bobbie stood up and said, "Yesterday, I told you I only have two jobs: ensuring safety and making money for the company. I told you I don't have time for ideas because I am completely busy as it is. But then I had to do my homework assignment. So, I called in someone from the plant who is always pestering me with ideas. I told her to meet me for breakfast this morning and come prepared to give me an idea.

"I bought her breakfast, and then I said, 'Okay, give me your idea.' I had the homework sheet on how to make a POINt evaluation right in front of me. She launched into her idea about how to manage plant safety training. To be honest, that's been a problem for us. It's taken far more time than it should. Well, I told her two positive things about her idea. I told her some opportunities. Then I phrased my concerns about the idea: 'In what ways might *you* get this done, because *I'm* way too busy to do it myself?'

"Well, I'll be darned if she didn't have an answer to that. A good one. 'Boss,' she said, 'I've already got this ready to go. All I need is your approval so I can implement it.' Do you know what? We're going to start saving $5,000 every two weeks by implementing this idea. I asked Blair to let me go first this morning because I want to tell you here and now that I'm going to start using this POINt evaluation every time someone brings me an idea." Everybody laughed and clapped. They all knew Bobbie. She was as good as her word.

Blair smiled. "Don't get ahead of yourself," he said. "Before you start saying you're going to save $5,000 every two weeks, you might want to verify that."

Bobbie looked Blair dead in the eye and said, "Miller, if there's one thing I know, it's how much everything costs in my plant. When I say it's going to save $5,000, you can take that to the bank."

• • • •

Practicing Praise First
can help you as a
leader **to set the climate
for how ideas are
going to be treated.**

A Father Makes a Good POINt
. . . .

Blair loves to hear people tell their stories about using Praise First. They are so shocked when the POINt evaluation works, and amazed to find how broadly it applies. You can use a POINt evaluation in project management to capture lessons learned, to conduct a performance review, to provide feedback, or to compare competing solutions. And it works just as well outside work as inside.

Blair once gave the same POINt homework assignment to a group of managers at a health insurance company. A man who was quiet on the first day of the course arrived early the next morning and asked to share his POINt evaluation first. The group took their seats.

"I need to preface this by saying that I'm a single parent," he began. "My wife died three years ago, and in many ways I haven't gotten over the loss. My son is in high school. It's just him and me trying to make this work, and sometimes it's a struggle.

"Last night, after the training, I came home late, feeling exhausted. I pulled the car into the garage, and the first thing I saw was that the trash had not been taken out. That meant another week with full gar-bage bins. One of my son's few jobs is taking out the trash. And I've got to tell you, I was upset. Really upset. I went into the kitchen, and all that I could think were bad thoughts about my son, how ungrateful he was, how selfish, how he has just this one job.

"Ten minutes later, he walked into the house, looking upbeat, and it struck me, this is exactly the moment Blair was talking about, the moment when I was ready to lay into someone with criticism, but instead, I could use Praise First and do a POINt evaluation. My first thought was, 'What am I supposed to say? Something good about not taking the trash out?' Then it struck me: All I could think about were awful things to say, and he's the reason I'm alive. I do everything for him. My wife would want it to be so. At that moment, I chose to try Praise First.

"'I got a letter from your coach,' I told him. 'Coach says you're really not the best player on the team, and he wishes he could start you, but he can't. But he absolutely wants you on the team. What he values is that at practice you give it your all, every day. He said that you're an absolutely invaluable member of that team because that rubs off on the other players.' I was getting ready to tell him something about the opportunity when he interrupted me.

"'Dad,' he said, 'something has been on my mind all day. It wasn't until I got to school that I realized I didn't take the trash out today. I am so sorry. It's just, in the morning, I am so tired, it's all I can do to throw some food in my mouth and get to school on time. I genuinely forgot. And I know, it's my one thing to remember.'"

The man stopped his story for a moment and looked up at the class. "At this point, this was the longest conversation my son and I had had in three years." He teared up. People around the room quietly reached for their own tissues. "I asked my son, 'What might be some ways we could get you to remember that?' And together, we sat around the kitchen table and generated a list of things that might work."

CREATIVE PROBLEM-SOLVING tools can help people go after big challenges without going after each other. Practicing Praise First can help you as a leader to set the climate for how ideas are going to be treated, and how the team as a whole is going to interact with performance, ideas, and evaluations. You may worry that a POINt evaluation will take too much time or that, if you say anything good about an idea, it means you're endorsing it. In reality, neither of those ends up being the case. With practice, you can do a POINt evaluation in the same time you'd take to do any other evaluation—but with fewer hurt feelings and better results. Because when you can genuinely see something good about someone's idea, they end up being more open to the issues you raise to improve it.

The next time you need to give feedback or respond to an idea, hold your fire. Ask yourself, What simple, true thing can I say to let them know I see them, I value them, I recognize what's good about their idea, and I'm here to help? Then use Praise First and offer a POINt evaluation.

Now we've loaded you up with tools to handle the cognitive challenges that come your way, but what about the emotional ones? That's your next challenge.

GOOD IDEA
RESPONSE

BAD IDEA RESPONSE

··12··

Navigating Blowups and Breakdowns

A
T THE END of the team meeting, Frances asked everyone to stay until the conference room was cleaned up, but instead Craig took a phone call and disappeared, ignoring her request and leaving everyone else to do the work. As the new team leader, Frances had to show her authority by holding him accountable. She resented being put in that position.

Why the heck did he leave like that? She started imagining stories in her head. Did he fake that phone call just to get out of cleanup duty?

The next morning, when Craig walked into the office, Frances started ribbing him. "Hey Craig, where were you yesterday when the rest of us were cleaning up the conference room?"

Now Craig, who had just been publicly shamed, was defensive. Frances, who felt her authority had been undermined, was posturing, and everyone else was staring fixedly at their computers, trying to be invisible, waiting for the bad feelings to pass.

EMOTIONAL UPSETS happen at the most surprising times—and over the most surprising things. You can be sitting around having a perfectly normal meeting when suddenly negative emotions escalate. A trapdoor opens, and it's as if the whole conversation falls down a rabbit hole and is now taking place against unfamiliar, potentially hostile scenery.

At times like these, evolution has conditioned us to react with one of three responses:

- **Flight:** you try to escape. *I'll deal with it later. Much later.*
- **Fight:** you fight back. *No, YOU'RE an idiot!*
- **Freeze:** you ignore it. *I'm sure he didn't mean that.*

As a team leader, none of these natural responses will serve you well. So, what's a body to do?

Well, first, don't listen to your body. Your evolutionary programming should not be in charge at a moment like this. When our emotions run hot, we shift our problem-solving headquarters from our rational neural networks to our emotional ones. If you "let it all out" now, there's a good chance the stress hormones coursing through your system will erase the fine line between letting it out and lashing out.

Instead, pull from the meditation playbook. Don't react. Notice. Be present to what just happened. Assume it was not about you. (Even if it was about you, this is not the time to make it all about you.) If you feel yourself having an emotional reaction, take a slow breath. As meditation experts will tell you, breathe in through the nose and out through the mouth. Let the emotion drain out. This may require a few breaths. Then be curious.

You are endowed with the extremely useful gift of being able to wedge a moment of awareness between a rising emotion and your reaction to it. If you can pause in that moment, instead of being taken over by the urge to fight, take flight, or freeze, you can choose another way.

Mistakes Will Be Made

Learn to simply notice your natural reaction and gently bring your focus back to the present. The goal is not to eliminate all negative emotion in yourself or on your team. The goal is to be at ease with whatever comes—to stay calm and present amid the turmoil so you can help yourself or your team navigate through.

"People are frightened of emotions," says Tom Ross, a Chicagoland psychotherapist with thirty years in private practice. "Emotions can feel out of control and inefficient, so having emotions at work seems inappropriate. The problem is, if you have people at work, you have emotions there too." Hiding them does not get rid of them. Repressing them does not make them go away. They end up sneaking back in in ways that are even more twisted, bizarre, and disruptive.

"We've pathologized emotions, especially in business," Tom continues. When emotions come up, we tend to run. "It's a natural reaction, but if you run from emotions on a team, your team never fully develops. You stay in the forming stage and never brave the emotional turmoil of the storming stage. And if you don't go through storming, you don't come out the other side into norming and performing."

Your Thinking Preferences Show Up in Your Emotions

Negative emotions are not a sign of a bad team, but they are a sign that something needs to be addressed. Think of them as a flag on the field. They call for a pause in the action so people can speak their truth and be heard.

Curiously, emotional upsets can show up differently, based on someone's thinking preferences.

Under stress, people who prefer to clarify tend to disengage. When there's no clear direction, instruction, or intention, they simply pull out. You can see it in their body language. They fold their arms and step away from the group, unwilling to waste time and energy on actions that have no strategy. Disengagement is a sign of emotional upset.

Under stress, people who prefer to ideate tend to emote. If people can't see the big picture, if leaders impose arbitrary rules, or if others fail to understand their brilliant idea, these usually easygoing, playful people can get mad, dramatic, or upset. If you handle the issue, they are likely to restore to their usual lighthearted selves just as quickly.

Under stress, people who prefer to develop tend to get critical. When others fail to build robust systems or don't give them the building blocks to construct a successful solution, they can become critical, caustic, and nitpicky, and find fault in everything and everyone.

Under stress, people who prefer to implement tend to take over. When they encounter resistance, they get louder and more insistent. They seek more control. They try to take charge and become more autocratic.

You don't have to follow your natural instincts when emotions arise. As Frances gained more experience, she learned not to call people out publicly to show dominance. Now, if someone does something she doesn't understand, she resists the urge to make up stories, ascribe evil intent, or trump up character flaws. Once she's calm, she takes them aside and asks what happened, using the following approach.

Situation Behavior Impact (SBI)

The Center for Creative Leadership trains some of the world's top executives. One of the things they teach leaders is how to respond to breakdowns, using a feedback method called Situation Behavior Impact (SBI). When someone has broken trust or failed to hold up their side of an agreement, they teach leaders to wait until they are calm and present, then open a channel of communication. Choose a psychologically safe setting and ask if the person has time to talk. Begin by identifying the exact situation, so there's no confusion. Point to the specific behavior and explain the emotional impact it had on you. Only then do you ask what happened.

Now, let's see how SBI might work in the situation with Craig and Frances.

Situation: Narrow the focus to a specific situation, saying when and where it took place.

● ● ● ●

**You are endowed with
the extremely useful gift**
of being able to wedge
a moment of awareness
between a rising emotion
and your reaction to it.

Craig, do you have a minute? I wanted to speak with you about what happened yesterday afternoon, at the end of our team meeting when I asked everyone to stay and help clean up.

Behavior: Describe the specific behavior you observed in nonjudgmental terms.

You took a phone call and left the room.

Impact: Share the emotional impact it had on you. Ask the other person to share their intent, then listen.

I felt ignored. Can you help me understand what was going on for you?

At this point, Craig told Frances that the phone call was from the nurse's office at his son's school. His son had fallen off the monkey bars and possibly broken his ankle. Craig had to race him to the emergency room. That phone call from the school nurse chased every other thought from his head. He apologized to Frances for running out on the team.

On hearing what actually happened to Craig, all thoughts of faked phone calls vanished from Frances's head. "I'm so sorry!" she said. "How's your son? How are you?" If she had only known the real story, she would have been the soul of compassion from the beginning.

Good leaders aspire to be compassionate, whether they know the story or not. They operate with the assumption that, at any given time, people are doing the best they can. It may not be good, but it's the best they've got—at least at that moment. When people fall short, use the Situation Behavior Impact method to gently surface their story. Learn what really happened. Understand their intent. It keeps you from filling in the blanks with stories of your own making.

Good Feedback, Bad Feedback

One of our most embarrassing traits as human beings is that we naturally ascribe negative intent to other people's behavior and positive intent to our own. That's why the SBI method is so difficult to follow. When you're secretly sure you've been wronged, the last thing you want to do is show emotional vulnerability. You don't want to admit, "I felt ignored." It's easier to blame your negative emotions on someone else: "You ignored me in front of the whole team."

The hardest part of following the SBI method is keeping the impact part judgment free. It's hard to give good feedback and be vulnerable about how you feel. It's easier to give bad feedback and explain how they made you feel. This is how that might look:

Good Feedback	Bad Feedback
I felt stupid.	I felt like you made me look stupid.
I felt disrespected.	I felt like you showed no respect.
I felt sad.	I was saddened by your behavior.
I felt unhappy.	You made me unhappy.

Wonder whether you gave good feedback or bad feedback? There's a simple way to tell the difference.

In good feedback, you own your emotions, which tends to evoke compassion in others.

In bad feedback, you make others responsible for your emotions, and people instantly get defensive.

If team members can speak their truth in a productive way, that helps the team connect. Emotions and breakdowns often link to something you don't currently understand. In some ways, they are gifts, and you need to be ready to accept them.

When you approach breakdowns with curiosity and compassion, you often learn something important about the individual, the team, or yourself. Giving feedback is only the first half of the SBI method.

• • • •

When you approach breakdowns with curiosity and compassion, you often learn something important about the individual, the team, or yourself.

The second half is listening. After sharing the situation, behavior, and impact, ask, "Can you help me understand what happened?" Then listen generously. You may be surprised.

As psychotherapist Tom Ross explains, "When someone is upset, just the act of listening can help them feel safe. Even if you're the one who triggered the negative emotion, you can help by creating a safe space for them to be heard." As we learned in Chapter 6, if you do this one thing well—listen—you'll deepen trust and strengthen the relationships on your team.

Most of us have been raised to value privacy and politeness. So, we hold back on telling others the effect their actions have on us. But feedback is necessary to build honest relationships, clear the air, or help someone modify destructive behavior. Remember, your purpose should always be to help the receiver—and the team.

Teach your team the SBI method of giving feedback so they have a good tool for addressing the emotions and breakdowns that naturally happen at work.

Debrief for the Win

On a good team, everyone has the tools they need to effectively solve challenges—including emotional challenges. Any breakdown is a chance to learn. As a leader, if you're too quick to mothball the problem, people won't learn from it. Instead, after you've had time to reflect on what you've learned from listening, reconnect with the individual or group. Here's how to debrief what happened.

Ask the individual (or the group, or yourself)

- What went well?
- What would you do differently?
- What did you learn or relearn?
- What learning will you apply next time?

NOW THAT you can help your team navigate through not only intellectual challenges but emotional ones, you've got a complete set of moves to lead a good team. In the next chapter, you'll see how one leader brought all the moves you've learned in this book together to turn bad teams into good ones and transform subpar performance into outstanding business results.

- -

ACTIVITY
Give Good Feedback

- -

PROVIDING GOOD FEEDBACK is a way to tell people how they affect you and others. That information is powerful and sensitive. Do it with care, using the following guidelines.

Be direct. Talk to the receiver and not others. Offhand remarks have little value.

Be specific. General statements like "You don't listen" don't help much. Instead, tell people the specific things they say and do that cause negative reactions (e.g., "Just now, you interrupted John"). This focuses the issue more clearly.

Describe behavior, not personality. When you say things like, "Obviously, your commitment to this team is not very high," this is a statement about personality and motivation. It will probably raise defenses and make the other person less able to hear your feedback. Instead, try saying, "Yesterday, you disappeared when the room needed to be cleaned up." This describes the specific behavior that caused trouble and gives the person something to respond to.

Own your feelings. Say "I feel inadequate," not "You make me feel inadequate." Express your feelings rather than make accusations. But be wary: Any sentence that begins "I feel that you..." is not likely to be followed by the actual feeling. Begin instead with "I am (upset, annoyed, disappointed, etc.) when you (do this or that)."

Be aware of tone. If your tone is harsh, even your honest, straightforward feedback may come off as condescending or mean.

Time it. Feedback is most useful when given as soon as possible, based on the person's readiness to listen. Forcing an opinion on someone who is not ready to hear it is futile.

Limit information. Focus feedback on what a person can use or do something about. Overwhelming a person reduces the possibility of them hearing and acting on feedback.

Check communication. Ask if they understand what you mean. Confirm that your words are heard in the way you intended.

Balance negative with positive feedback. If your feedback is negative, provide supportive comments too, either at the time or later.

Like any skill, giving good feedback takes practice, practice, practice.

••13••

Your People Can Solve Any Challenge

LL HER fellow executives knew that Angelina was not afraid to handle the hot potatoes. She had a reputation as a turnaround leader in the company. She could take a dysfunctional group of leaders or an underperforming business unit and turn it into a productive team. Like her peers, she was driven, smart, and accomplished. But she also seemed to have a secret for turning bad teams into good ones.

You already know her secret.

Angelina discovered FourSight when she was in charge of a marketing team in Hamburg, Germany. The team was responsible for strategy and marketing of a $1.8 billion portfolio across the European region. It was truly an international group with eleven nationalities and nearly as many languages and cultures. The cultural diversity on the team, which was supposed to be an asset, had become a barrier to collaboration. How could Angelina help such a diverse team find a common language to understand each other at a deeper level?

Her leadership coach, Laura Barbero-Switalski, suggested using the FourSight Thinking Profile assessment with her team. Laura is a creativity expert who cofounded an annual creativity conference in Europe called CREA. She knew the power of FourSight to create a common problem-solving language among people of diverse cultures.

Blair and I are fans of Laura and CREA. When we asked her to share a story of team leadership, she immediately thought of Angelina, and she insisted that Angelina tell it in her own words. She said, "But Sarah, when you talk with her, I just want to underscore that you will be speaking with somebody who has brought impressive business results to every franchise she has ever led. She is an extremely talented, intelligent, smart, strategic leader."

Note to self: be on best behavior.

As a freelance writer, I've interviewed lots of executives. Could Angelina be so different? Was she some kind of dragon lady? I was a little nervous when joining our three-way Zoom call, but Angelina was the picture of graciousness. Her direct gaze definitely announced an executive presence, but her opening question revealed a mindset of empathy, inclusion, service, and problem solving. "How might I make this valuable for you?" she asked.

Definitely not a dragon lady. Definitely not a typical executive either. For the next hour, Angelina told stories about the teams she had served, with Laura adding color commentary. They had worked together, as leader and coach, on five different teams in different business units and on different continents. Over the years, they had developed a true friendship, and their mutual respect was obvious.

With Laura's help, Angelina turned the multicultural group in Germany into a high-performing team. Her success won her a promotion, a new assignment to run the leadership team in Eastern Europe. This team had an even bigger cultural challenge—and a bigger business one too.

Angelina described the cultural complexity she met there. "We tend to think about the people in that geographical area as one, but they are very different cultures. Some of these countries had been at war with each other. There were some very fresh memories. We had meetings where we couldn't seat people from certain countries next to each other. So, how do you create a common vision, a team spirit, when there are so many scars coming from historical events?"

Before her arrival, the individuals on the leadership team had managed their work very independently. "There was not a vision of how to operate as a team," she said. She knew the FourSight Thinking Profile would help them develop a common language. "The power of a common language is incredibly effective at creating alignment," she said.

She had recently discovered that thinking preferences also linked to creative problem solving. "That was a gem," she said. Now she could bring her teams not only a common language but a common process. "It became a powerful tool to solve apparently unsolvable business challenges."

She started to use thinking preferences to help her team anticipate where they would lose energy in the problem-solving process. Her leadership teams often preferred to ideate and implement. They would get enthusiastic about a new idea and want to rush it to implementation. Angelina recognized their low energy to develop as a potential blind spot. So, she established a practice of doing a POINt evaluation before they implemented any solution. That simple tool helped them spot issues that needed to be addressed and improved business outcomes.

"Applying FourSight was magic," she said. It took some time, and was not without difficulties, but as the common language took hold, she saw the transformation begin. "People started to feel things like, 'We can get together as a team. We can accomplish greater things for the overall benefit. We can learn from each other. And if we apply our resources collectively, we'll get more value back.'

"It was beautiful to see the change—and the business impact," said Angelina. "When I took on the business, it was really underperforming. The first year was a hard year. We couldn't achieve our business goals, but we created these foundations. We started with the senior leaders and spread it to the next two levels. They would be the ones taking on the real projects and having to implement them. That's when we honestly created a cultural movement across the different countries."

For the next two consecutive years, Angelina was confidently leading the fastest-growing region in Europe. She said, "All these leaders were really transformed by the experience."

Change Is Hard (on Some People)

Transformation sounds great, but change is hard when it happens to you. And it's harder on some people than on others. Belgian organizational consultants Ingrid De Clercq, Karen Peirens, and Lara Donners recognized that thinking preferences might play a role. They developed the following preferences and suggestions to anticipate how people might react to change and what they would need to embrace it.

People who like to clarify will tend to see problems and pitfalls. They'll take a wait-and-see attitude, as a way to hold on to what is. They'll ask clarifying questions: Why change? Why this change? Is this logical? Is it final? Who's involved? Can it still be adapted?

They need: Facts, detailed information, "proof" that the change is a good thing and will be all right, a chance to ask questions, a methodical approach, and time to adjust.

People who like to ideate often welcome change. They like the idea of a new start and see the upsides. They adapt easily and are flexible, but may secretly (or publicly) think they have a better idea and want to contribute it.

They need: A vision of a better future, the bigger picture, an opportunity to add their own ideas, a chance to play with options and perhaps adapt the plan, and a way to start experimenting quickly.

People who like to develop often react cautiously and sometimes anxiously to change. They want assurances about the quality of the solution and its implications on the context. They may even question the need for change, preferring to improve the current solution.

They need: A clear understanding of the need for change: What elements have made it necessary? Is it logical? They also need time to think, evaluate, and adapt systems to accommodate the change.

● ● ● ●

Transformation
sounds great,
**but change is
hard when it
happens to you.**

People who like to implement tend to accept change easily. They are ready to jump into action and try it immediately. They want quick feedback on whether it works. They may push others to move forward and get impatient when they don't. They themselves may become negative or resistant if they can't leap into action quickly enough.

They need: An explanation of why the change is good for them specifically, to be involved, to start implementing immediately (albeit on minor tasks), to have action plans, time schedules, and deadlines.

CHANGE WAS Angelina's bread and butter. With Laura as her coach and FourSight as her secret weapon, she helped five teams transform. "The fact that I used it for ten years, on five different teams, across many geographies really is a testimony of its adaptability—from a cultural, geographical, and business standpoint."

What Angelina didn't expect was that she herself would be transformed in the process. FourSight became a natural and pragmatic way for her to develop empathy. She found that, through the lens of thinking preferences, she could understand people who think differently. She was less irritated by teammates who challenged her. "I've learned over the years that people don't necessarily want to win. They want to be heard. They want to contribute. If you give them the experience that you are really listening, that you see things from their perspective, then they will respect you, even if you don't agree with them.

"I always had a bias for ideation and implementation. Looking back, what was difficult for me, and many leaders, was to accept the vulnerability that you're not perfect in all dimensions. You need to be okay with that. One of the ways I evolved as a leader was this acceptance."

Eventually, it went beyond the acceptance. "I was thriving with that awareness, saying, 'Okay, these are the things I'm doing well. This is where I need your help.' On my last team, my finance person was a great clarifier. I would go to him and say, 'You're stronger than me at this. Help me ask the right questions and define the right problem so we can create ideas, knowing exactly what we're solving for.' As a leader, if I didn't show that I accepted my gaps and my vulnerabilities, I couldn't expect others to do so."

As Angelina grew more self-aware, she achieved results more quickly. "Part of it was my confidence in the tools, which allowed me to delegate and empower people much faster. It was a pleasure to watch them build on each other's strengths. It took less of my intervention."

The unintended consequence of her success was that Angelina got promotions that landed her all the hot potatoes. "You start creating that team spirit, that cohesion, that feeling of being unstoppable, of being able to solve every challenge," she said. "Then you end up solving the challenge, and you get a reputation. So, guess what? The next job you get is another hot potato!" She inherited businesses with big troubles from a compliance, integration, business results, portfolio, or innovation standpoint. "There was always something that other leaders had tried to solve unsuccessfully. Now here is the magic lady who is going to come and solve it. You create this reputation of being a transformation leader, and you end up getting more and more difficult challenges. But the fact is, it worked. If I want to communicate one thing to other leaders, it's the business impact."

WHAT COULD you learn from Angelina? How might you take the wisdom of team leaders, coaches, researchers, consultants, and teams and make something that works for your own team? In the final chapter, we'll leave you with some ideas.

••14••

Flip the Coin

E *PLURIBUS UNUM.*

It's the Latin phrase printed on every coin and dollar bill in the United States. It means "out of many, one." It's the de facto motto of the United States. It's the ideal that has made this country uniquely powerful—bringing diverse people together to do something bigger than any of us could do alone.

E pluribus unum is the only Latin phrase I ever memorized, aside from *Semper ubi sub ubi*, which my next-door neighbor Heidi taught me meant, "Always wear your underwear."

We can walk through this life alone or together. Now that you know the recipe for how to make a good team, you can choose to do it together. You can deliberately pull together the ingredients of purpose, trust, and process; harness people's thinking preferences; and tackle big challenges. Together.

Good teams will help you achieve big goals, but they are more than a means to an end. The ability to connect with others to solve real challenges creates a bond, a sense of belonging and purpose that is its own reward. Good teams are sustaining.

In high school, I played field hockey at University Liggett School, a small private school in Grosse Pointe, Michigan. Muriel Brock was our coach. She was legendary. In her career, she coached nineteen undefeated seasons—not winning seasons, *undefeated* seasons. She was tough. She had high standards. She made us work impossibly hard. Players came from every social clique, grade, and academic level in the school to play as a team. We loved our goofy bus-ride rituals. We loved our tattered mouse mascot, Mickey. We alternately loved and were terrified of Coach Brock.

Mostly, we loved field hockey.

My neighbor Heidi was our star halfback. Senior year, we went undefeated in Michigan, so we flew to Connecticut to play the "real field hockey teams" in Greenwich and Darien. We flew home, still undefeated. That season, we scored seventy-one goals, with three goals scored against us.

I went on to play field hockey in college. It was okay. I liked the people, but the long practices and bus rides didn't seem worth the time commitment. That's when I realized I didn't actually love the game of field hockey. I loved being on Coach Brock's team. I quit field hockey and joined the ultimate Frisbee club team.

Once you are part of a good team, you know what's possible. The memory never leaves you. Forty years after our high school graduation, I got a call asking if I'd give the speech to honor Heidi's induction into our high school's athletic hall of fame. Of course! A small crowd had gathered in the side cafeteria. Coach Brock was there. Now in her late eighties, she had the same piercing gaze, leathery tan, and shock of white hair, but her voice was shaky, and it cracked unexpectedly mid-sentence. "It's from yelling at [crack] you girls all those years," she rasped, shaking her head in mock chagrin. Then she grabbed me and Heidi in a vise-grip hug and sat in the front and watched with an eagle eye as I began my speech.

> Having Heidi as a neighbor was like winning the lottery. She was game for anything. We climbed trees, made forts, and rescued baby bunnies. When we started playing field hockey, our relationship changed from playmates to teammates. I noticed something would happen to Heidi whenever she braided her hair and tied on that red bandana. No more bunny-loving Heidi. She became Attila the Halfback.
>
> A similar transformation, albeit not quite as pronounced, happened in all of Coach Brock's players. We'd be singing cheery songs on the sidelines, but when that whistle blew, we were all business. Field hockey

was one of the only places where girls were allowed to be unapologetically fierce and fast and aggressive. We were proud to be known as the "Brocksketeers." Today, I run a business. Many of the skills I use to win in the market came straight from field hockey. I'm a businessperson and an entrepreneur, but in my heart, I'm still a Brocksketeer.

I stole a glance at Coach Brock. She was dabbing her eyes with her paper napkin. Score. Being part of a good team makes you realize that the secret of life isn't the "why" or the "what," it's the "who." Muriel Brock was the team leader who made all the difference. She inspired me to help start a field hockey team at our local high school. I wanted to create a space where other girls could be strong and have a true sense of connection. As recounted in Chapter 8, we started out as the worst team in the league. Nearly a decade later, I'm still coaching field hockey, watching individual players transform into a team. This year, our team made it to the state Final Four championships, but our purpose is still the same: to give every girl a good team experience. We want being part of our team to be one of their best memories of high school.

THINK BACK. Who is the team leader who made a difference for you? Who provided a space where you could push yourself, work with others, and be great together? How might you do that for others?

In a world where technology promises limitless connections, we have never felt more disconnected. The freedom of remote work can leave us feeling disengaged. Global conflicts, climate change, and politics cause disease, dislocation, distrust. That's a whole lot of "dis" happening. "Dis" comes from the Latin word meaning "lack of, apart, asunder, in a different direction." In a world that's never been more connected, we've never felt more "dissed."

But you now have the tools to change that, at least in your own team. You can articulate a clear purpose, build trust, and lead an inclusive problem-solving process. It doesn't matter what kind of team you lead. It can be a work team, a volunteer committee, a kids' sports team, a short project, or a lifelong mission. If it's a group of people who take on challenges together, you have an opportunity to make it a good team.

The Good Team Challenge
. . . .

What would the world be like if every person had the chance to be part of a good team? How might you be part of that movement? Let's think that through.

To clarify, it's harder now than ever to make a good team. Remote work has fractured our sense of connection. Job turnover constantly disrupts the cycle of team development. Technology keeps handing us more and more complex challenges. And don't forget thinking preferences, which continue to trip us up at every turn.

How might we lead good teams with the people we have? (You can see the problem-solving path I'm following here.)

Let's ideate on the possibilities. What if you could align people with a clear purpose, get to know their hopes and fears, and give them a common language to solve complex challenges? What if you tried this at work? At home? Or with the volunteer committees that you serve?

Develop a plan. Maybe you see yourself learning more about what each person on your team cares about and what challenges they need to help them grow. You may learn about each other's thinking preferences so you can collaborate more effectively. You may set time aside to clarify your team purpose and even create a team charter. You may build trust and connections by taking on meaningful challenges and use a shared problem-solving process to solve them. You have the moves now to fight back against the "dis" and join a movement to build good, respectful, meaningful, purpose-driven teams that make the world a better place.

What I like about that. It's a damn good challenge. It's worth your time. It's a transferable skill. If you can do it with one team, you can do it with another. It might even allow you to spend your days solving more goal-oriented challenges and fewer people problems. It might help you collaborate with people whose problem-solving behavior baffled you in the past.

• • • •

Once you are part
of a good team, you
know what's possible.
**The memory
never leaves you.**

How might I begin? Start small. This is one of those "ten-thousand-step journeys." It's not going to happen overnight. But it won't happen at all if you insist on being amazing at it. Good is the goal. Do something good. Pick one thing from these pages that strikes you as promising and try it. If it works, you'll be one step closer to leading a team that everyone wants to join, a team that knows how to tap everyone's best thinking and solve almost any challenge. Together.

BLAIR AND I wrote this book with a clear purpose: to help you lead a good team. Thank you for the time you've dedicated to reading it. As you've probably realized by now, this is more than a business book, it's our life's work. We hope it's been valuable to you. I'll leave you with a story. It's not the story of a billion-dollar business or a top corporate executive. It's the story of a single leader who, against all odds, chose to make a good team.

The Ultimate Demotion

In his thirty-plus-year career, Dennis Carter had worked nearly every job in the Buffalo manufacturing plant where his father and his grandfather had worked before him. He was two years from full retirement, and he'd finally gotten his master's degree and landed his dream job in organizational development. Then came the corporate downsizing.

Pink slips were flying. Dennis's dream job was eliminated by corporate mandate.

The plant manager knew that Dennis had a wife on permanent disability, and that he needed two more work years to get the medical coverage that only a fully vested retirement package could give him. He offered Dennis the only job he had left: manager of the night shift for the waste management crew. It was the ultimate demotion. The people on this team were notorious. They were folks with attitude problems, the ones who had been rejected from every other position in the plant. This was their last stop before being fired, which was almost guaranteed to happen to them in the next downsizing.

Dennis took it as a challenge. He'd studied the creative problem-solving process. He knew how to create a good team. He set out to get to know every person on the team, their strengths, their hobbies, their stressors. He knew who had kids, mortgages, boat payments, and alimony payments.

Then he sat them all down as a group and leveled with them. "We all know the score," he said. "When the next downsizing comes, you'll all be out of a job. No paycheck. No health insurance. No benefits. These are the brutal facts. How many of you want to leave?"

Nobody raised a hand.

"Wouldn't it be great if this team were seen as an important part of running this plant?" There was nervous laughter. These people knew they were expendable in the eyes of corporate. "Well, that's my goal," he declared. "And there are some simple things I want us to do.

"First, whenever people call down to waste management and ask for something to be done, I want you to say, 'We'll take care of that.'" He was stealing a page right out of the Four Seasons customer service handbook. "No request is out of bounds," he continued. "It's always 'yes, how can we help?'

"The purpose of this team is to solve problems," he told them. "On the call, you don't need to commit to what you're going to do, or when. Bring that to the group. We'll figure it out together."

Dennis hung a whiteboard in his office and waited. Slowly, team members began to show up with challenges. He didn't solve them. Instead, he helped them think through each problem. "People like to solve problems," he said. "Take that away from them and they hate it. Leadership is allowing people to solve their own challenges."

As team members' confidence grew, so did their trust in Dennis. Before long, the notorious third shift was transforming its reputation. People on the team were developing a sense of pride in their work.

By the time two years was up, Dennis was confidently leading a high-performing team, full of people the organization had once deemed most likely to fail. He did it by combining purpose, trust, and process. At the next downsizing, not a single member of the third shift waste management crew got laid off. And Dennis? He retired and moved with his wife, Betty, to their dream house in the north woods. He left on a high note, having fully vested in his retirement, and fully vested in his team.

The world is full of challenges—global, occupational, personal. What are yours? The big ones? How might you create a good team when the stakes are high, the chips are down, and the outcome is important?

This book represents the collective wisdom of many. What you learned here can help you lead a good team. But these are not just leadership skills, they are human skills. Yes, they can help you lead a good team. They can also help you lead a good life. They don't require you to be extraordinary or amazing. They just require you to do the work—to flip the coin and manifest the motto. Out of many, one.

Acknowledgments

IT WON'T surprise you, although it still surprises me, that this book was the creation of a team. I don't just mean me and Blair—who's still my favorite teammate. I mean the thriving teams that enrich our lives—namely, our children and extended family, whose support was unwavering; our McPark neighbors, who still invite us to social gatherings even though writing this book has made us antisocial for nearly two years; our all-weather tai chi team that keeps us both grounded and transcendent.

Thank you to our FourSight partners: Gerard Puccio, Greg Sonbuchner, and Russ Schoen, an extraordinary team of thinkers. And to the rest of our fabulous FourSight team, including Kelly Roberts, Christine Long, Jitendra Rai, and Ashish Kumar, and the hundreds of professional trainers, facilitators, teachers, researchers, and consultants who have dedicated their careers to bringing creative problem solving, collaboration, and FourSight to people around the world.

To the faculty and staff of the Center for Applied Imagination at SUNY Buffalo State University, including Roger Firestien, Susan Keller-Mathers, Molly Holinger, Jo Yudess, Kristen Peterson, and David Yates, whose teaching, facilitation, and research are a source of continuous inspiration. And to Selcuk Acar, whose research and thought partnership helped transform FourSight from an assessment into a theory.

To AJ Harper, who taught us to write a better book in her Top Three Book Workshop, and to Laura Stone, who, along with AJ, cracked the code for how to make writing a team sport. To Mike Michalowicz, for introducing us to a new level of book writing (and to AJ).

To our early readers, including Orrin Murray, Judy Reid, Doug Reid, Abby Wilkymacky, Dorte Nielsen, Sophie Tversky, Kari Lindemann, and Doug Philipsen, whose warm enthusiasm carried us over periods of doubt. And to Jonathan Vehar, whose knack for clarifying always brings us closer to our goal.

To the talented publishing team at Page Two: Sarah Brohman, Taysia Louie, Louise Hill, and Ashley Rayner, all led by the inimitable Trena White and Jesse Finkelstein. You are the embodiment of a good team!

To all the teams and organizations that have invited us to work with them and given us a firsthand chance to learn and practice our craft. We are grateful to you as our teachers.

If you enjoyed this book or found value in it, you can thank those teams. We do.

Finally, to our readers: thank you. You are the ones who carry this forward and manifest it in your own teams, organizations, and communities to make the world a better place.

Notes

Introduction

p. 5   *discovered a scientific way to measure cognitive style differences:* Puccio, G. (1999). Creative problem solving preferences: Their identification and implications. *Creativity and Innovation Management, 8*(3), 171–78. doi.org/10.1111/1467-8691.00134.

1: Your People Problem Starts with You

p. 14   *team leaders are often chosen because:* Adkins, A. (2015). Only one in 10 people possess the talent to manage. Gallup. gallup.com/workplace/ 236579/one-people-possess-talent-manage.aspx.

p. 16   *productive teams need three things:* Climer, A.E. (2016). *The development of the creative synergy scale.* PhD diss., Antioch University. aura.antioch .edu/etds/270.

2: Trace Collaboration Breakdowns to the Source

p. 30   *you need four different types of thinking to solve a complex challenge:* Puccio, G.J. (2002). *FourSight: The breakthrough thinking profile (Presenter's guide).* THinc Communications.

p. 30   *you like to work with people who share your thinking preferences:* Goodwin, A. (2018). Exploring cognitive styles to examine explicit theories and implicit perceptions within teams. Unpublished PhD diss., University of the Virgin Islands.

p. 31   *Let's take these four stages one at a time:* Miller, B., J. Vehar, R.L. Firestien, S. Thurber, and D. Nielsen. (2011). *Creativity unbound: An introduction to creative process.* FourSight.

p. 38   *the following quiz, originally published in the* New York Times: A version of this quiz appeared in print in the *New York Times* on February 9, 2014, on page 8 of the quarterly Education Life, with the headline "What Kind of Thinker Are You?" nytimes.com/2014/02/09/education/edlife/what-kind-of-thinker-are-you.html.

3: Go from "Hands-On" to "Hands-In" Leadership

p. 43   *See if you recognize any of these behaviors in the following table:* Puccio, G.J., B. Miller, and S. Acar. (2019). Differences in creative problem-solving preferences across occupations. *Journal of Creative Behavior, 53*(4), 576–92. doi.org/10.1002/jocb.241.

p. 46   *Thinking Preferences among Leaders* [chart]: Proprietary data set from Thurber, S. (2023). FourSight Database/set/November-2023. For the interested reader seeking an in-depth look at leaders in organizations, see Puccio, G.J., and S. Acar. (2015). Creativity will stop you from being promoted, right? Wrong! A comparison of creative thinking preferences across organizational levels. *Business Creativity and the Creative Economy, 1*(1), 4–12. doi.org/10.18536/bcce.2015.07.1.1.02.

4: How Good Leaders Think

p. 58   *concept of teacher's pet may actually be connected to thinking preferences:* Gurak-Ozdemir, S., S. Acar, G. Puccio, and C. Wright. (2019). Why do teachers connect better with some students than others? Exploring the influence of teachers' creative thinking preferences. *Gifted and Talented International, 34*(1–2), 1–14. doi.org/10.1080/15332276.2019.1684221.

p. 65   *In her TEDx Talk, she poses a provocative question:* Cahen, H. (2022). The new golden rule for high performance collaboration. TEDxSeattleStudio. youtube.com/watch?v=hCpN4fSDKGg.

p. 65   *cognitive diversity has the biggest impact on performance:* Reynolds, A., and D. Lewis. (2017). Teams solve problems faster when they're more cognitively diverse. *Harvard Business Review, 30*, 1–8. hbr.org/2017/03/teams-solve-problems-faster-when-theyre-more-cognitively-diverse.

5: Teams Work on Purpose

p. 79   *identified purpose as one of the three things a productive team needs:* Climer, A.E. (2016). *The development of the creative synergy scale.* PhD diss., Antioch University. aura.antioch.edu/etds/270.

p. 82   *leaders who prefer to clarify enjoy a higher level of trust among followers:* Puccio, G., S. Jahani, and T. Garwood. (2022). The impact of leaders' creative problem-solving preferences on teams. *International Journal of Innovation, Creativity and Change, 16*(3), 57–81. ijicc.net/images/Vol_16/Iss3/16233_Puccio_2022_E1_R.pdf.

6: Trust Me

p. 92   *people who worked at high-trust companies reported:* Zak, P.J. (2017). The neuroscience of trust: Management behaviors that foster employee engagement. *Harvard Business Review, 95*(1), 84–90. hbr.org/2017/01/the-neuroscience-of-trust. See also Zak, P.J. (2017). *Trust factor: The science of creating high-performance companies.* AMACOM.

p. 93   *Gallup ran an engagement study that revealed three things:* Gallup study data summarized in Smith, M.M. (2015). Ignoring employees: It wreaks havoc on your team and bottom line. TLNT. tlnt.com/ignoring-employees-it-wreaks-havoc-on-your-team-and-your-bottom-line/.

p. 93   *psychologists recommend a six-to-one ratio of praise to criticism:* Brown, W.E. (1972). Praise–criticism ratio: Do teachers take advantage of it? *Behaviorally Speaking,* 5–8.

p. 95   *the more skillful the leader is at listening:* Zenger, J. (2022). The unforeseen rewards of good listening. *Forbes.* forbes.com/sites/jackzenger/2022/05/19/the-unforeseen-rewards-of-good-listening/?sh=2c5634886645. See also Kluger, A.N., M. Lehmann, H. Aguinis, G. Itzchakov, G. Gordoni, J. Zyberaj, and C. Bakaç. (2023). A meta-analytic systematic review and theory of the effects of perceived listening on work outcomes. *Journal of Business and Psychology,* 1–50. doi.org/10.1007/s10869-023-09897-5.

p. 98   *Project Aristotle, Google's famous team study:* Duhigg, C. (2016). What Google learned from its quest to build the perfect team. *New York Times Magazine.* nytimes.com/2016/02/28/magazine/what-google-learned-from-its-quest-to-build-the-perfect-team.html.

p. 98   *high performance requires the openness, flexibility, and interdependence:* Edmondson, A.C. (2008). The competitive imperative of learning. *Harvard Business Review, 86*(7–8), 60–67, 65. hbr.org/2008/07/the-competitive-imperative-of-learning. An update to this is worth checking out: Edmondson, A.C. (2018). *The fearless organization: Creating psychological safety in the workplace for learning, innovation, and growth.* John Wiley & Sons.

p. 101 *Edward Deci and Richard Ryan's research on motivation:* Deci, E.L., and R.M. Ryan. (1985). *Intrinsic motivation and self-determination in human behavior.* Springer Science+Business Media.

7: Speed the Path to High Performance

p. 104 *identified distinct stages of team development:* Tuckman, B.W. (1965). Developmental sequence in small groups. *Psychological Bulletin, 63*(6), 384–99. doi.org/10.1037/h0022100.

p. 108 *how thinking preferences affect people's confidence in others:* Goodwin, A. (2018). Exploring cognitive styles to examine explicit theories and implicit perceptions within teams. Unpublished PhD diss., University of the Virgin Islands.

8: Create a Climate for Teams to Thrive

p. 125 *identified ten dimensions that affect team climate:* Ekvall, G. (1996). Organizational climate for creativity and innovation. *European Journal of Work and Organizational Psychology, 5*(1), 105–23. doi.org/10.1080/13594329608414845.

9: Teams Need Challenges

p. 133   *the* New York Times *Spelling Bee:* Takahashi, D. (2023). How the *New York Times* is building a games platform around Wordle. *GamesBeat.* venturebeat.com/games/how-the-new-york-times-is-expanding-into-puzzle-games-like-wordle/#:~:text=All%20told%2C%20the%20 New%20York,millions%20of%20players%20every%20day.

p. 133   *making progress, even a little progress, on hard goals makes people happy:* Amabile, T., and S. Kramer. (2011). *The progress principle: Using small wins to ignite joy, engagement, and creativity at work.* Harvard Business Review Press.

p. 134   *teams and challenges have a symbiotic relationship:* Katzenbach, J.R., and D.K. Smith. (2015). *The wisdom of teams: Creating the high-performance organization.* Harvard Business Review Press.

p. 134   *the kinds of challenges that many of us have to face in work and life:* Snowden, D.J., and M.E. Boone. (2007). A leader's framework for decision making. *Harvard Business Review, 85*(11), 68. hbr.org/2007/ 11/a-leaders-framework-for-decision-making.

p. 134   *you may experience a positive state of "flow":* Csikszentmihalyi, M., S. Abuhamdeh, and J. Nakamura. (2014). Flow. In *Flow and the foundations of positive psychology: The collected works of Mihaly Csikszentmihalyi,* 227–38. Springer Science+Business Media.

p. 135   *the challenges you face will inevitably get harder as your level of leadership rises:* Mumford, M.D., S.J. Zaccaro, F.D. Harding, T.O. Jacobs, and E.A. Fleishman. (2000). Leadership skills for a changing world: Solving complex social problems. *Leadership Quarterly, 11*(1), 11–35. doi.org/10.1016/S1048-9843(99)00041-7.

p. 137   *lists the ten job skills essential for success in the coming years:* Di Battista, A., S. Grayling, and E. Hasselaar. (2023). *Future of jobs report 2023.* World Economic Forum. weforum.org/publications/the-future-of-jobs-report-2023/.

p. 144   *ways to build and sustain cross-generational innovation teams:* DeCusatis, C. (2008). Creating, growing and sustaining efficient innovation teams. *Creativity and Innovation Management, 17*(2), 155–64. doi.org/10.1111/ j.1467-8691.2008.00478.x.

10: The Secret to Better Solutions

p. 147   *broaden their study of psychology beyond mental dysfunction:* Guilford, J.P. (1950). Creativity. *American Psychologist, 5*(9), 444–54. doi.org/ 10.1037/h0063487.

p. 149   *Divergent thinking is a core leadership competency:* Vincent, A.S., B.P. Decker, and M.D. Mumford. (2002). Divergent thinking, intelligence, and expertise: A test of alternative models. *Creativity Research Journal, 14*(2), 163–78. doi.org/10.1207/S15326934CRJ1402_4.

p. 151   *groups trained to separate divergent and convergent thinking:* Puccio,
G.J., C. Burnett, S. Acar, J.A. Yudess, M. Holinger, and J.F. Cabra. (2020).
Creative problem solving in small groups: The effects of creativity training
on idea generation, solution creativity, and leadership effectiveness.
Journal of Creative Behavior, 54(2), 453–71. doi.org/10.1002/jocb.381.

11: Power Tools for Problem Solving

p. 160   *start your question with a phrase that invites new thinking:* Miller, B.,
J. Vehar, R.L. Firestien, S. Thurber, and D. Nielsen. (2011). *Creativity
unbound: An introduction to creative process.* FourSight. For a bit more,
see: Firestien, Roger. (2023). *Solve the real problem: Because what you
think is the problem is usually not the problem.* Green Tractor Publishing.

p. 163   *you must master the skills of creative problem solving:* Mumford, M.D.,
S.J. Zaccaro, F.D. Harding, T.O. Jacobs, and E.A. Fleishman. (2000).
Leadership skills for a changing world: Solving complex social problems.
Leadership Quarterly 11(1), 11–35. doi.org/10.1016/S1048-9843(99)
00041-7.

p. 164   *Praise First, the POINt evaluation tool:* Miller, B., J. Vehar, R.L. Firestien,
S. Thurber, and D. Nielsen. (2011). *Creativity unbound: An introduction
to creative process.* FourSight. The predecessor of POINt was a tool called
PPC, which examined pluses, potentials, and concerns of an idea. PPC
was originally developed in the early 1980s by Diane Foucar-Szocki, Bill
Shephard, and Roger Firestien.

12: Navigating Blowups and Breakdowns

p. 175   *emotional upsets can show up differently:* Ackerbauer, M. (2020).
Examining the relationship between creative preference and social style
behavior. Unpublished PhD diss., University of the Virgin Islands.

p. 176   *a feedback method called Situation Behavior Impact (SBI):* Bommelje, R.
(2012). The listening circle: Using the SBI model to enhance peer
feedback. *International Journal of Listening, 26*(2), 67–70. doi.org/10
.1080/10904018.2012.677667.

13: Your People Can Solve Any Challenge

p. 188   *They developed the following preferences and suggestions:* De Clercq, I.,
K. Peirens, and L. Donners. (2013). FourSight and dealing with change.
CONGAZ presentation for Digipolis. Bruges, Belgium.

About the Authors

THE AUTHORS of this book are married. And we're still married, even after writing this book together, which is a testament to how well this stuff works. We hope it helps you and your teams take on big challenges and end up even better together.

 **SARAH THURBER** is an author, speaker, entrepreneur, and team leader. As managing partner at FourSight, she has led a diverse team of experts to develop ways to empower teams to embrace their unique strengths and enhance performance. Thurber works directly with academic researchers, professional facilitators, technical leaders, and designers to spearhead the development of online and print-based tools that support cognitive diversity and creative problem solving. She is coauthor of *The Secret of the Highly Creative Thinker: How to Make Connections Others Don't* as well as many popular FourSight training manuals and resources.

BLAIR MILLER, PhD, is cofounder and partner at FourSight and president of Blair Miller Innovation. For three decades, he has combined team-building and problem-solving facilitation to help teams create new products, patents, and strategic plans. He codeveloped a business simplification process that led to more than $1.8 billion in savings for Fortune 500 clients like Mars and Kraft. Miller has coauthored influential training manuals, published academic articles, and received the Distinguished Leadership Award from the Creative Education Foundation. He is an adjunct professor at the Center for Applied Imagination at SUNY Buffalo State University.

BECOME PART OF THE GOOD TEAM MOVEMENT

• • • •

· ·

**Start your "Good Team" leader journey
and meet other leaders on the path.
Sign up for free webinars and inspiration
at foursightonline.com/good-team.**

· ·

BRING FOURSIGHT TO YOUR TEAM

Discover your thinking preferences and equip everyone to think creatively, work collaboratively, and solve challenges more effectively. Book a workshop at **foursightonline.com/team-workshops.**

HIT THE RIGHT KEYNOTE

Inspire your organization to think better together and book a keynote by Sarah Thurber or Blair Miller. Find out more at foursightonline.com/keynotes.